AN ARENA OF TRUTH

ALSO BY TERENCE CLARKE

Novels:
My Father In the Night
The King of Rumah Nadai
A Kiss for Señor Guevara
The Notorious Dream of Jesús Lázaro
The Splendid City

Story Collections:
The Day Nothing Happened
Little Bridget and The Flames of Hell
New York

Non-fiction:
Fathers, Sons, and Seizures

AN ARENA
OF TRUTH

Conflict in Black and White

~ Terence Clarke ~

A/T
—Publishers—

ISBN (paperback edition): 978-1-7329195-0-1
ISBN (ebook edition): 978-1-7329195-1-8

Published by A/T Publishers.
756 Bay Street, Suite A, San Francisco, California 94109 U.S.A.

To contact the author, please visit http://www.terenceclarke.org.
Requests for appearances by the author and/or Dr. Peter Kranz are welcome, as are requests
for educational and library pricing.

Cover design by Ashley Ingram (http://www.ashleyingramdesign.com)
Photo of Terence Clarke by Nancy Dionne (http://www.nancydionne.com)

This book is a work of non-fiction.

In memory of
Dr. Price M. Cobbs

Not everything that is faced can be changed, but nothing can be changed until it is faced.

—James Baldwin

Unless a person is made to feel uncomfortable, he doesn't move.
—A black student in the class "Human Conflict: Black and White"

TABLE OF CONTENTS

FOREWORD

Dr. Price M. Cobbs

In recent years, as each new racial firestorm has erupted and been featured on the national news, I have noticed a familiar cry for help. Whether involving a single black person and a single white person, or groups of both, and no matter how complicated or simple the situation, the same earnest suggestions and shopworn remedies are offered. Whether endlessly discussed by the chattering class on cable television and social media, by panels of notables in public forums, or taking place in private discussions at a dinner table, in a coffee shop or office, the resulting conclusion remains invariably the same. Someone, somewhere, states solemnly that the time has come for America to have "a conversation about race."

The particular incident may have been a trigger-happy cop confronting an unarmed black man, a white saleswoman dissing a hapless black shopper at a local Walmart, or a headline in the local paper about gang-related murders in the inner city. It may be a story about black students walking out of a high school over a perceived racial slight, or a white law school applicant suing because he wasn't admitted, while a presumably less qualified black applicant was accepted. Whatever "it" is, if race is involved, somehow a "conversation about race" becomes a must.

In reality, however, the conversation remains long-delayed or short of the mark once it does take place. It is invoked as a way to understand, soothe, or otherwise temper the effects of whatever incident might indeed have occurred. Somehow it seems that, if people have this conversation, they will understand things more fully, resolve the particular issues and, in the process, have more respect for each other and their different perspectives.

Whether intended or not, the frequency with which this "conversation about race" is proposed implies that it is the go-to cure, the magic pill that, if ingested, will promote greater understanding about race and racial issues.

But here, now, I ask the reader to take a deep breath.

Conversations can be a good thing. They can be fruitful. Many times they have a positive outcome. But it is a baffling idea to reduce a situation to a simple "conversation about race," when the situation is centuries old, and involves slavery, emancipation, Jim Crow laws, personal and institutional racism, societal presumptions of white superiority and corresponding black inferiority.

In my lifetime there have always been conversations about race. As a black adolescent doing what youngsters of my day did, we talked about it quite a bit. The one unstated rule then was that such discussions were limited to our own, black, group. I always assumed that many Whites might have been having similar discussions, limited to their own groups. The only time in my experience that the conversations were broader was during the occasional panel discussion in college or at a conference, with the obligatory multi-racial faces quietly discussing race. In later years I came to call such conversations "eggshell discussions", in which everyone walked softly even as the actual situations that had fostered the conversations had so clearly been fraught with peril, real and presumed, on both sides.

Under discussion in such panels, the reactions to the actual peril remained subdued and carefully controlled, through politesse, good manners, and very strict ground rules.

The focus then and now was on tolerance, understanding, and acceptance by Whites of Blacks, and by Blacks of Whites. There was, and unfortunately still is, an underlying belief that we are all really the same regardless of our external appearances. The discussions invariably end with everyone professing that the world would be better off were we to become "color blind," whatever that phrase may mean.

This groundbreaking book about Dr. Peter Kranz and his students tells a different story. Theirs is a remarkable tale of how more direct, sometimes even combative, noisy, and very aggressive argument can indeed lead to long-term positive results in the racial divide and lifetime commitments to each other among the participants. Pete attended a group in San Francisco in 1970, at the height of the Civil Rights Movement. It was lead by Bill Grier and me. We had recently published *Black Rage,* and the tremendous reception to our book pushed us to go further than simply writing about race. We developed a model for a racial confrontation group for mental health professionals from around the country, and it was this group that Pete attended.

We wanted the group to go beyond the platitudes and niceties that substitute for real understanding. Our work with patients had taught us how the attempts of black and white Americans alike, in their wishes to understand themselves and the world around them, are inevitability filtered through prisms of gender, culture, social standing, economics, and many other things. But race is the one circumstance that pertains to all Americans. To ignore any one of these other elements is to miss what makes people tick, what makes them similar, and what makes them different from each other. But we had found irrevocably that to pussyfoot around race in any such discussion is to ignore the single most important element of them all.

And pussyfooting, in "conversations about race," was the norm.

Little did we know in 1970 that the group Pete participated in was to provide a significant addition to his early idealism and a starting-point for what he was eventually to accomplish. For much of his academic career at a variety of educational institutions, Pete has organized classes and conducted groups aimed at helping his students think about, and feel much more deeply, the state of race in this country. This book shows his and his students' courage as pioneers and meticulous architects in the development and implementation of an *authentic* conversation about race.

—San Francisco, California

–1–

A SHORT PREAMBLE TO 1972

The classic wooden ax handle can be a formidable weapon. Even without the murderous addition of the iron or steel ax head, the handle, wielded without mercy in a fight, can do terrible damage to the person being attacked. It is heavy. The wood is thick and has substantial weight. The handle is about three feet long and, if used against someone who cannot defend against it, it can kill.

In 1960, Jim Crow laws that had disenfranchised black people in the South of the United States—if not in some respect in every state of this country—were more or less in full flower. After the end of Reconstruction in 1877, these laws had been instituted systematically across the southern states. They were arbitrary, unfair and completely discriminatory. They were also very effective in keeping a lid on what large numbers of the white populace in the South viewed as a dangerous rise in the political power of black people. In their minds, any such rise was to be quashed. If you were black in most of the South, you couldn't vote, public and private facilities were segregated, as were the schools, your housing was the worst, employment opportunities somehow evaded you, and you were stuck.

With the integration of the armed forces in 1948, the Supreme Court decision of Brown vs. Board of Education in 1954, and various other court decisions and legislative programs, the situation for Blacks had improved. But no one would dare claim that the foundations of Jim Crow in the South had been seriously shaken.

Jim Crow was filled with ironies. One of them was that, if you were black, you could now freely shop in many white-owned retail establishments, especially the big ones owned by corporations. They valued your money, and took it. But if you wished to have bacon and eggs at the lunch counter of any of those stores, and you were black, you were consigned to a second-class lunch counter that served Blacks only. The lunch counter for Whites was off limits to you. If, after having shopped in the store and spent your money, you felt that this kind of treatment was unfair, you were free to take your business elsewhere.

By 1960, these lunch counters had suddenly become targets for civil unrest on the part of, and demonstrations by, black people who were very un-amused by the fact that they could not have a meal in the same way that white people could. Like those Whites, they had left significant moneys in the coffers of the particular store. But sitting next to a white person and enjoying a tuna sandwich…that was beyond the pale. As James Baldwin wrote memorably, "All of Africa will be free before we can get a lousy cup of coffee."

On February 1, 1960, four black students from the North Carolina Agricultural and Technical College in Greensboro sat down at the white lunch counter of the Woolworth's store in that city, and asked for menus. When they were refused service, they refused to leave. Dressed pristinely in coats and ties, polite and quietly straightforward in their behavior, they stayed at the lunch counter until the store closed. They did not get served. The manager of the store, a white man named C.L. Harris, said, "They can just sit there. It's nothing to me."

The next day, a larger group of black students arrived at the white Woolworth's lunch counter, and the same quiet impasse developed. National news organizations had been notified of what was happening, and the Greensboro "sit-in," as it was called, became a news phenomenon. Suddenly, white shopping establishments across the South were being visited by well-dressed, quietly expressive young Blacks who, when refused service at the white lunch counters, remained at the counter until the store closed. The sit-in had become almost instantaneously a very newsworthy occurrence in the South.

On the morning of August 27, 1960, Arnett Girardeau, a black student home in Jacksonville, Florida for the summer from Howard University

Dental School, went to Hemming Park in the downtown area with a few others, having gotten some news of potentially alarming activities there. "As we approached Hemming Park, we saw several white men wearing Confederate uniforms. Other Whites walked around Hemming Park carrying ax handles with Confederate battle flags taped to them. A sign taped to a delivery-type van parked [nearby] read 'Free Ax Handles.' Small fence rails bordered that section of Hemming Park. We could see bundles of handles in the shrubbery. No one attempted to conceal them."

A group of young black students from the local NAACP Youth Council were planning on sitting in that day at the white lunch counter in Jacksonville's own Woolworth's, which was walking distance from Hemming Park. The first such event had taken place two weeks earlier, when eighty-four of the youths sat down at that counter and waited to be served. The counter seated exactly eighty-four people, so there was no room in this instance for a white person looking for lunch. (This was part of the plan for all subsequent sit-ins in Jacksonville. The number of seats in whatever lunch counter would be assessed, and exactly that number of black youths would show up for the sit-in.)

In the case of these Woolworth's sit-ins, the Blacks at the counter were ignored. As planned, they had purchased a few items each from the store, so that they could claim legitimately to be customers. Two of the students, Alton Yates and Rodney Hurst, were the "captains" of that first sit-in team. Their requests to be served were turned away by a white waitress, who offered the suggestion that "the colored lunch counter is at the back of the store." The students stayed put, and eventually the Woolworth's manager closed the lunch counter.

Rodney Hurst, wanting to see the reaction to what the students had done, combed the next day's edition of the *Florida Times-Union*, the local white-owned newspaper. There was no mention of the sit-in.

The same number of students came back downtown on August 27, a Saturday. They had planned yet another demonstration at Woolworth's, when Arnett Girardeau learned of the surreptitious delivery of ax handles to the shrubbery of Hemming Park. After a strategy session, the Youth Council demonstrators decided not to sit in that day at Woolworth's; rather to sit in at the white lunch counter at another establishment, the W.T. Grant department store. This was simply a safety ploy, an effort to avoid the violence they felt they could encounter if they returned to Woolworth's.

Despite this care, they did encounter trouble, and it was not benign or gentle.

Once the demonstrators sat down at the W.T. Grant lunch counter, the store's management immediately closed the entire store. Hurst, writing later in his book *It Was Never About A Hotdog And A Coke*, described what happened next: "When we came out of Grant's...we could see in the distance a mob of Whites running toward us. As the mob got closer, it became obvious they were swinging ax handles and baseball bats. In a surreal scene, they swung those ax handles and baseball bats at every Black they saw."

The black community heard about the ensuing dispute even as it was going on, and scores of them descended on the downtown district, to help protect those being attacked. Prior to the arrival of this assistance, there had been very little police presence in the area. Once black people in significant numbers arrived, however, the police arrived as well.

The battle was on.

It went far into the night. Radio stations warned white people to stay out of black neighborhoods, and vice versa. In one particularly memorable event, a truckload of armed white men (believed to have been Ku Klux Klansmen) arrived in a black neighborhood called Blodgett Homes, and began firing at various apartments. Perhaps to the surprise of these men, residents of the apartments returned fire. The truck retreated.

In later years, there were other, more apocalyptic such skirmishes elsewhere in the country, which became the stuff of contemporary history: the Watts Riots in Los Angeles in 1965, in which thirty-four people were killed; the Twelfth Street Riot in Detroit in 1967, in which forty-three people died and 1,189 people were injured, along with 7,200 arrests; the riots in Los Angeles in 1992, after a jury exonerated three of the four arresting police officers from having committed any crimes in their savage beating of a black taxi drive named Rodney King. Fifty-three people died in those riots, and 2,383 were injured.

The day of the 1960 Jacksonville events became known as "Ax Handle

Saturday", and it remains a signal occurrence in the history of civil rights in the United States.

—

In 1959, a new public high school had opened its doors in Jacksonville, Florida. It was named after Nathan Bedford Forrest, a Confederate lieutenant general who had become the first Grand Wizard of the Ku Klux Klan. All the students at the new school were white.

In 1963, George Wallace became governor of Alabama. A white man, he declared in his inauguration speech, "In the name of the greatest people that have ever trod this earth, I draw the line in the dust and toss the gauntlet before the feet of tyranny, and I say segregation now, segregation tomorrow, segregation forever." Later that year, Wallace protested the admission of black students to the University of Alabama, and President John F. Kennedy ordered the U.S. Army's 2nd Infantry Division, from Fort Benning, Georgia, to be prepared to enforce the admission process. Wallace famously blocked the door to the main auditorium of the university, although he was quickly hustled away by soldiers who had been ordered to do so in person by Nicholas Katzenbach, the deputy U.S. Attorney General at the time.

On June 12, 1967, the Supreme Court nullified anti-miscegenation laws in Florida, one of the last states in America where people could go to jail for marrying across racial lines.

In the 1968 national election, Wallace, now a third-party candidate for president of the United States, won a majority of the votes in Jacksonville, Florida.

On Halloween afternoon, 1969, a white man was making a delivery of cigarettes from his truck to a Jacksonville store when, he later alleged, he saw a black man attempting to get into the truck. The deliveryman ran back out to the street, pulled a pistol, and shot the black man in the leg. A crowd gathered, mostly black people, and the police were called. When they arrived on the scene, they found a group of young Blacks moving down Florida Avenue, near the downtown shopping area. Many of the young men attacked stores, which were owned principally by white business people, and the ensuing violent police roundup lasted until seven o'clock that evening. Over the next two days, further instances of violence resulted in more damage to buildings and more looting. The police came back. Four buildings were torched, thirteen people were arrested, and one storeowner died of a heart attack in the middle of the fracas.

These difficulties did not go unheeded by the city government. Various committees and commissions were founded, to determine the truth of what was happening and, more important, the underlying reasons for why the events were taking place. It was suggested that "a conversation about race" should be held.

To be sure, though, there remained difficult negative attitudes among the citizenry. White people unsympathetic to the advances of their fellow black citizens obdurately continued opposing what they believed to be unacceptable race-mixing and the social threat posed by Blacks, who were now far more enabled by federal legislation to make their own way. In the decade before 1972, black people had won the right to dine at integrated lunch counters throughout the city. Schools were being desegregated. The 1965 Voting Rights Act had opened the door to Blacks who wished to vote and had not previously been permitted to. Much that was positive was indeed happening, despite the lingering, deeply felt hard feelings toward each other between most black and white citizens.

In 1970, Jacksonville was the largest city in the United States not to have a state university campus. To rectify this situation, one thousand acres of a natural preserve were set aside, a few miles south of the downtown, for a new higher education facility. It was named the University of North Florida, or UNF, and its doors opened in the fall of 1972. Students attending the school in those early years often joke about how, on the way from the parking lot to their morning class, they had to keep an eye out for alligators. The first graduating class—thirty-eight students—matriculated in June 1973.

The university had hired a young professor with a PhD in Child Psychology from Utah State University. Peter Kranz arrived in Jacksonville for the opening 1972 semester, and noted that the university's curriculum was itself in a state of flux and development. Pete was white and Jewish, from New York City originally, and was well attuned to the continuing stressful state of race relations in the United States. He had arrived at North Florida having undergone a few important and emotionally challenging events in his own life, with regard to race. UNF was a new school. It seemed to him to be an open-minded place. He felt a unique opportunity to bring to the university a program in the study of race in the U.S., the likes of which no full institution of higher learning had ever attempted.

Pete Kranz was thirty-two years old.

–2–

PETE AND MICKEY

As a boy, Pete Kranz had a friend named Mickey Schwerner. They were children of liberal New York Jewish families long friendly with each other. A pair of 1946 photographs shows the boys at a New York City playground, both six years old, a baseball bat clearly being readied for use in a kids' pickup game. They are enjoying a couple bottles of Coke. It's a warm day, Pete dressed in a striped T shirt, Mickey in short-sleeved plaid, both in jeans. Pete's are probably newer than Mickey's, since the cuffs of his are rolled up thickly, no doubt in preparation for what his mother suspects is a coming growth spurt. The photos have a Norman Rockwell-esque sincerity about them, two boys ready to play ball on a bright summer day. If the reader knows what New York City looks like, he'll find recognizable territory in the background buildings of one of these photographs. These are small boys from the Big Apple.

As they grew up and went off to school, Pete and Mickey remained in occasional contact, and Pete recalls a conversation they had in 1964, when they were in their mid-twenties. Mickey had recently married, and he and his wife Rita came in one day to the store in which Pete was working a part-time job. The two young men talked, glad to see each other. Both had been attending universities, and both had been watching with avid interest the unfolding of the Civil Rights movement everywhere in the United States. A federal legislation was being debated in Congress at the time—what was to become the Civil Rights Act of 1964—and it was the most sweeping such legislation to have been considered in the twentieth century. It was not, however, the first such legislation, although it rested firmly on the same ground with the presidential emancipation proclamation made into law on January 1, 1863, and the subsequent passage of the Thirteenth Amendment to the U.S. Constitution.

—

The long history preceding those two events was singularly difficult, since it began with the sale of the first black slave in the colonial North American territories, in 1619. The debate between the slave territories—later slave states—and those states that did not permit slavery is itself a very major element in the history of the new nation. Eventually that debate came to a head in the disastrous civil war that began on April 12, 1861.

The prosecuting of that war eventually provided President Abraham Lincoln with a unique opportunity to change the entire conversation.

At the Battle of Antietam on September 17, 1862, fought near Sharpsburg, Maryland along the nearby Antietam Creek, the Union army pushed Robert E. Lee's forces back, after this first fierce full-army battle on northern territory. The carnage was complete. Twenty-seven thousand soldiers died that day. The Union victory was pyrrhic, since the Union General George McClellan did not pursue Lee's Confederate forces once they had been turned back, thus giving them the opportunity to retreat to Virginia, to fight another day. But for President Lincoln's purposes, a win was a win, and five days later he made the preliminary declaration of a proposal to free all slaves from the warring Confederate states. Effectively this meant even more than the removal of the chains of slavery from black people. The proclamation also allowed former slaves to join the Union's armed forces, and two hundred thousand of them did.

The Emancipation Proclamation became official on January 1, 1863, and was followed almost two years later by the adoption of the Thirteenth Amendment to the U.S. Constitution. Slavery had been abolished.

The southern states were not going to take all this lying down, however. From the end of the Civil War until 1877, the South was governed by representatives from the victorious North, or by southerners who had been anti-slavery advocates or, at most, only moderate supporters of the Confederacy.

To ensure the peace, many thousands of Union soldiers were stationed throughout the South. In the meantime, other issues had taken the national attention: the Indian Wars in the West; the impeachment trial of President Andrew Johnson in 1868; the scandal-ridden difficulties of the administrations of President U.S. Grant; the Financial Panic of 1873, among others. Reconstruction in the South began to lose its sense of political urgency. Numbers of Reconstruction officials (often called by those who hated them "carpetbaggers" if they were from the North or "scalawags" were they from the South) seemed to conservative southerners to be far too radically liberal in their sentiments toward the millions of freed slaves.

By the election of 1876, a kind of exhaustion had set in, and the presidential contest itself resulted in an electoral bargain that had sweeping consequences. Rutherford B. Hayes, a Republican, had won the electoral college plebiscite by one vote. But voting irregularities in three states had brought this result into serious question. An electoral commission was therewith formed, comprised of eight congressional Republicans (the party of Hayes) and seven Democrats (the party of rival candidate Samuel Tilden.)

The election was awarded to Hayes by this commission. It is generally conceded that the Hayes forces, wanting a clear mandate, offered the Tilden backers the promise that federal troops would be withdrawn from the South if the Democrats would give up their opposition to Hayes. The South would therewith regain control of its own destiny. With the subsequent agreement, Rutherford Hayes became president, and Reconstruction was brought to a swift end.

Accepting the compromise, the Republicans (the party of Abraham Lincoln himself) abandoned its quest for racial equality in the South, and in 1877 Hayes indeed withdrew the troops.

It would be impossible to re-instate slavery, though, given the Thirteenth Amendment. So southern politicians began a reconstruction of their own, by passing state and municipal laws that discriminated heavily against the black citizens of the South. Over many decades, this re-imposition of flagrant legal barriers resulted in a grand framework of such laws throughout the region that finally won the name of "Jim Crow."

The figure of Jim Crow himself was nothing new. A character from

American minstrel stage and song, he had long been portrayed as an addled, clumsy black man, a figure of abrasive comedy and gross disrespect. Laughable. Stupid. A "colored" dunce. As most famously embodied during the 1830s in a minstrel act by a white performer (made up in black face) named Thomas Dartmouth Rice, "Jim Crow" had been famed for singing lyrics like these: "Wheel about and turn about and do just so./Every time I wheel about, I jump Jim Crow." Among white minstrel fans, Jim Crow was a nationwide favorite.

After 1877, a dizzying avalanche of laws was imposed upon black people in the South (as well as, to a much lesser degree, in the North), laws that remained on the books well into the second half of twentieth century. These were the Jim Crow laws. The statutes were not intended to restrain serious criminal lawbreakers. They were more often cynical social restrictions intended to make all manner of normal behaviors criminal, when engaged in by Blacks. A study of the extent and reach of Jim Crow laws before 1964 is one that numbs the imagination. It seems that the one institution that remained un-recoverable by Jim Crow advocates was that of slavery itself. Every other kind of discriminatory restriction was theoretically permissible, if a particular state legislature or municipal government wished it to be so.

The Civil Rights Act of 1964 effectively began the dismantling of Jim Crow. Such prejudicial laws remained enforceable, although less effectively, through the following years. With time, they were reduced in power by the federal government's full implementation of the act and by use of the bully pulpit and, occasionally, the armed forces, by various presidents.

But in 1964 in the southern states, simply being black remained a dangerous condition. A full array of social restrictions still denied black people full rights as citizens. Most damnably, Blacks found it almost impossible to register to vote in elections. The Congress of Racial Equality, among other civil rights groups, instituted a program called "Freedom Summer," one purpose of which was to provide volunteers to go into black neighborhoods, urban and rural, in the South, to help black citizens register. Many of the participants of Freedom Summer came from outside the South, and this effort was resented by southern Jim Crow zealots, reminding them of the Reconstruction activities of carpetbaggers and scalawags a century before. Doing this work that summer, many of the volunteers understood the risks they were taking, of possible injury and confrontation. Few expected that their very lives might actually be in jeopardy.

—

"Mickey and Rita came into the store," Pete Kranz now recalls. "Just to say good-bye. It was nice, because we hadn't seen each other for a while." Mickey had entered a graduate study program at the School of Social Work at Columbia University in 1961. He had left the program in order to become a social worker in a Lower East Side housing project. Closely watching developments in the South, he and Rita had eventually decided that Mississippi was the center of the Jim Crow efforts to restrict black people in the South from voting. They decided to join the Congress of Racial Equality, and when they came into the store in which Pete was working, the couple was in final preparations to leave for the South. They spoke enthusiastically with him about what they were going to do.

At the time, Mickey was twenty-five years old.

By June of that year, he had become a voting registration organizer in Meridian, Mississippi. On the evening of June 21, he and two other members of the Congress of Racial Equality, a black man from Meridian named James Chaney and another white New Yorker named Andrew Goodman, were driving at night on a highway outside Philadelphia, Mississippi. They did not realize that the Ku Klux Klan's local "Imperial Wizard," Sam Bowers, had decided that Mickey's activities with local Blacks needed to be stopped. He and the two others were apprehended that night on that highway, by a white sheriff's deputy named Cecil Price and some others. The were taken to the jail in Philadelphia, Mississippi and, a few hours later, released to the custody of several white men who were members of the local KKK. Mickey, Andrew and James were murdered that night. Their bodies, which the killers had buried near a reservoir, were discovered forty-four days later.

When Pete learned from the television news about Mickey's initial disappearance, he was, of course, shocked and worried about his friend's possible fate. Pete and Mickey's parents were representative of a recognized concern among northern liberal Jews about civil rights in general. The Jews themselves having been discriminated against for eons (most sharply in the twentieth century by the Russians under Lenin and Stalin, and to be sure by the Germans under Adolf Hitler,) they had done much in the United States to assist the efforts of the black population to achieve full civil rights.

"I was raised on West Ninety-sixth Street in Manhattan," Pete says. "When you grew up in the city of New York, you had friends and colleagues from different ethnic groups. So, prejudice and discrimination against others was rarely even mentioned in our household…except to acknowledge that this or that event here or there was really unjust. We knew that such feelings clearly existed in this country, and we would talk about it around the kitchen table."

Pete's parents set the tone for those conversations at mealtime. "My mom was basically at home until we went away to school, but she had a degree in social work. And my dad was in Broadway theater as a stage manager. He worked with individuals of varied backgrounds, including those from the gay community. In our house, there never was an issue of what group you belonged to. Rather, it was the quality of the person, and the quality of the performance."

The family moved to Scarsdale, New York in 1951, and it was here that Pete encountered his first personal lesson in discrimination. "Restrictions. Prejudice. The Scarsdale Country Club did not permit membership for black people, nor did they allow Jews."

Pete followed the news of Mickey Schwerner's disappearance closely, and learned of the federal government's hunt for him and the others, and the investigation of their fate. "Mickey's disappearance and, especially, the later discovery of what had happened to him and his colleagues was a seed for me. I began to think, 'Let me see in the future what I might be able to do…how I could get involved.' What happened to Mickey was terrifying. Even so, it did not result in a volcanic flow of immediate action on my part. It provided nonetheless that seed that, with other elements, grew into ideas that I was later to nurture into a class in which I thought I could have a real and positive impact as an agent of change."

PRICE COBBS, BILL GRIER, AND CONFRONTATION

Throughout his studies in university, Pete Kranz read in the literature of, and thought deeply about, race in the United States. In 1970, he read one book in particular, by two black board-certified psychiatrists in California, which had received stellar, even amazed, reviews in the national press. *Black Rage* by Dr. Price M. Cobbs and Dr. William H. Grier was the first ever effort to understand the plight of black people in the U.S. from the trained psychiatric point of view of black physicians. Originally published by Basic Books in 1968 (within five years of the assassinations of President Kennedy, Medgar Evers, Malcolm X, Martin Luther King Jr. and Robert F. Kennedy) it immediately attained national best-seller status. It describes the long-term effects of slavery and Jim Crow on contemporary black people and, through many vivid character sketches of black individuals from every level of the economic spectrum, reveals in depth the psychological issues that accompany marriage, family, ambition, bereavement and, through all of these, the institutional discrimination that black people routinely encounter. Love, sex, sexual myths and misunderstandings... emotional dysfunctions, descents into depression and sometimes near-madness...all are described.

The book goes far into a study of racial hatred and its effects upon the black psyche. The authors tell of the instance of, and the damage caused by, mental illness among black people, and point out how the various manifestations of such illness can often be attributed simply to the effects of centuries-long discrimination. Finally, *Black Rage* ponders the future, and what Americans can expect if these issues are not specifically engaged, understood, and dealt with.

Drs. Cobbs and Grier laid out the situation in stark terms in the first chapter of *Black Rage*. "The growing anger of Negroes is frightening to white America. There is a feeling of betrayal and undeserved attack. White people have responded with a rage of their own. As the lines become more firmly drawn, exchange of information is the first casualty. If racist hostility is to subside, and if we are to avoid open conflict on a nationwide scale, information is the most desperately needed commodity of our time. Of the things that need knowing, none is more important than that all Blacks are angry. White Americans seem not to recognize it. They seem to think that all trouble is caused by only a few 'extremists.' They ought to know better."

Dr. Cobbs and Dr. Grier were indeed also studying the depths of white people's resentments against Blacks. The resentment is quite real, if not based in the same kinds of firm fact that has caused such pain in the psyches of black people. Although numerous immigrant groups have been discriminated against in the United States, and still are, there has seldom been as full-bodied a group of actual laws (i.e. Jim Crow) as there has been for Blacks, and Whites have gone on more or less unbothered personally, and unmoved, by *any* such thing. The two psychiatrists realized nonetheless that, before the racial crisis in this country could be faced and reduced, the anger in white people also needed to be dealt with. Their further studies convinced them that the solution, though potentially very difficult, was for Whites and Blacks simply to talk—directly—to each other.

But indeed it was not that simple. These two men knew that, at least since the Civil War, there had been numerous serious conferences, gatherings, and conversations between black people and white people, under the aegis of organizations like the NAACP, the Urban League and others, white and black, in which the divide between the two races had been discussed. These had usually been quiet, well organized, reserved and polite, on both sides. But "black Americans," the two physicians had written, remained "held tight in a snare, [having come] more and more to realize that even their inner suffering is due largely to a hostile white majority and, with this realization, [having gained] a determination to change that hostile society."

While they were writing *Black Rage*, the authors were developing a program that would bring black and white participants together, a program that was proving very effective in helping resolve, at least on an individual basis, the intertwined and ultimately dangerous interaction between Blacks and Whites.

In the same way that no book quite like *Black Rage* had ever been published, no solution to the difficulties between the races like the one Cobbs and Grier were bringing to the fore had ever been considered.

—

In March 1969, Drs. Cobbs and Grier proposed to the University of California Medical Center in San Francisco a new kind of gathering intended, as they described it in their proposal, "to provide a forum where people can examine thoughts, feelings and attitudes as they relate to race." On the face of it an entirely straightforward, unambiguous idea, these gatherings were yet given the name "Racial Confrontation Groups." The description in the Cobbs/Grier proposal of the groups' purpose clarifies the use of the word *confrontation*: "The experience can provide a setting where hidden and negative thoughts and feelings about different racial and ethnic groups can be fully explored."

The important idea in this description is that of full exploration. If the exploration is to be brought about by "confrontation", the results will ipso facto *not* be calm, vapid, or without intensity. Rather, they will be forceful and direct, potentially loud, and possibly quite difficult for those involved.

"We felt," Price Cobbs recalls, "that the social climate of this country at the time underscored the fact that feelings about race were a factor, no matter at school, work or anywhere. We recognized that there was a lot being said and written about the United States as a racist society with racist institutions. But there were few means for people to make these concepts personal."

The two psychiatrists were convinced that this lack of direct confrontation of the very real facts of race in this country was seriously damaging to the fabric of the society. One could talk calmly and politely about the racial divide forever. "For us, though," Cobbs continues, "thoughts about race and color permeated the self-perception of most Americans, and created stifling self-hatred and secret bigotry, as well as cruel prejudice and racial violence."

Drs. Cobbs and Grier proposed forming a group of a dozen or so people at the UC Medical Center, Blacks and Whites, to be overseen by two facilitators, one black, the other white. Gender balance too was a goal for the group. The group would meet over a period of two succeeding days, for ten hours per day. "Every attempt would be made to help participants make conscious their hidden feelings about the black experience and the white experience," Cobbs says. "And, most importantly, their feelings about each other. The group's interaction would be purposefully intense, and at times jarring, but always with the goal of healing rather than hurting."

In their proposal, the two psychiatrists described their specific goals: "Group discussions are directed beyond an exploration of abstract positions and concepts, and are aimed at immediate thoughts and feelings as they pertain to race. There is an emphasis on directness and honesty, and a focus on the here and now…. The aim is to help people understand their inner lives sufficiently, so that they may change their actions regarding race."

Confrontation was the method, and real understanding, by the participants, of the real problems between Blacks and Whites was the goal. It would be rough, Cobbs and Grier counseled the UC committee, and the one restriction was that actual physical violence would not be permitted. But the two psychiatrists knew that the method they had in mind was eminently workable and, in their eyes (given their experience in this kind of group, which they had initiated privately elsewhere) successful.

Cobbs and Grier had been organizing such groups at the Esalen Institute in Big Sur, California for two years prior to 1969. Esalen still exists and is a retreat center that does significant work in the development and dissemination of alternative and humanistic forms of education. In the 1960s, under the rubric of "Human Potential," such education aimed to bring about fresh ideas for, and actions to achieve, higher planes of understanding of the human psyche. Human Potential wishes to bring new levels of knowledge, self-acceptance, and self-avowal to the individual. One of Esalen's innovations was the use of small encounter groups—"T-groups," they were called—to study the nature of personal awareness, the difficulties of understanding such awareness, and the possibilities for achieving it.

Through their study of and participation in these kinds of groups, Drs. Cobbs and Grier had learned to use many of the processes of the human potential movement in new ways, their purpose being to lay bare the real issues of racial difference in the United States.

They made their proposal to Dr. Philip R. Lee, a white physician who had recently been named Chancellor at the University of California Medical Center campus in San Francisco, and a committee of other senior staff people. "These were deans and department heads, and they were far more receptive than I would have thought them to be," Cobbs remembers. "They felt the need to broaden their outreach at the medical center, to enlarge the applicant pool so that it would reflect the racial and cultural changes that were so clearly going on in California. And Phil Lee himself was very enthusiastic about our ideas."

The proposal was accepted by the committee, and the first of the racial confrontation groups took place on that campus in 1969. The participants were Dr. Lee himself and those others on the committee who had listened to the proposal. The group was led by Price Cobbs. One tenet of the proposal that could not be implemented fully was that of racial balance. "There weren't enough black senior staff at that time to come anywhere near an equal representation of Blacks and Whites in the initial group," Cobbs says. This fact was duly noted by Drs. Cobbs, Grier, and Lee, and all the other participants.

As this initial group proved successful in its goals, more were scheduled, and other participants were sought out. These too were for the most part professionals in the fields of psychology, education, and social work.

Pete Kranz was one of them.

—

In 1969, Pete had received his doctorate in Child Psychology from Utah State University. He had been hired by the Kern County Mental Health Services in Bakersfield, California, as a licensed psychologist. He had read *Black Rage* and, like so many others, discovered in its pages descriptions of life for black people that he would never have imagined previously. For him, the book was simply a revelation. He harbored the wish to meet Price Cobbs and Bill Grier, and one day, while reading a professional journal, he saw an advertisement for their confrontation groups at the University of California Medical Center in San Francisco. Immediately interested, Pete went to the mental health services supervisors, expressed his interest to them, and received their permission to leave work for a few days, to attend the group.

"This was after *Black Rage*, and basically, I wanted to see what Price and Bill were doing now," Pete says. "And this idea of the confrontation group fascinated me. I assumed that I would receive training to be a supervisor in a similar group that I could organize myself. And indeed the experience with them was fundamentally helpful to the later development of my own classes along similar lines."

The group was held in an office conference room on Sacramento Street in San Francisco. "There were about a dozen people, blacks and whites, men and women," Pete says. "Most of them came from what I would call the 'mental health component.' Professionals in the field."

Cobbs describes his experiences in these groups. As he did more and more of them, certain patterns emerged. "The first part of the first morning would be the usual kinds of things for any meeting. Introductions. Why each of the people there wanted to participate. And the ground rules, of course. Above all, no physical violence. No intimidation. No threats. Since we were dealing with issues that could be inflammatory, it was important to remember that we were professionals, and would treat the issues here, in the end, professionally."

Pete Kranz remembers that, for the first hours of conversation between black and white participants in his group, politesse seemed to be the rule. The conversation was direct enough, but there was not a lot of hostility voiced by one group against another. Rather, the participants seemed to maintain a kind of respectful decorum that was a form of feeling each other out. Who's who? Who believes what about race? Who seems sincere; who seems evasive? Everything was straightforward enough, and very polite.

"That's true for every group in the first hours," Cobbs says. "But with time, things would become more contentious, more confrontational. Until someone, invariably a black person, would say to one of the whites, 'Yes, I know what you just described, Teddy. But I don't know what the fuck that means.' He would lean forward and point at Teddy. 'You white folks are always making assumptions like that about us.' What was being said was one thing, the elements or 'facts' in what was being said. But the *way* in which it was being said was suddenly something new. At that point in the proceedings, the black people were always much more direct, much more candid with what they had to say. Louder. They would have come to a moment of pent-up internal rage, in which a voice inside the black person or persons would say, 'Okay, I'm interested in this, but let me just let you know about how goddamned angry I am about the way things are going in this country, or the way I personally have been treated out there. Or the way you just treated me with that stupid assumption you made.' Finally, these black people were in a setting in which they could tell the others exactly how upset they really were. And they let all of us know how angry they were, and why, with very real examples of the treatment they had received during their lives. Yes, a particular black person might be dressed in a coat and tie, wearing his professional mask, carrying his PhD or MSW with him proudly. But he's as angry as some other black man you might see who's been beaten up and bloodied in a police riot, and is now being interviewed on the six o'clock news."

Eventually, after a period of retrenchment into apprehension or embarrassment on the part of the Whites, during which they would be looking toward the group facilitators for some help or protection from this kind of verbal onslaught, things would change.

Cobbs describes what would follow: "The Whites would come to understand that what they were hearing was authentic, and also that nothing was going to get out of hand. And then, the balance of the conversation would shift, and the white folks would begin responding, often with similar raw feelings about things they felt they understood about black people. They had plenty of resentments, too, and this could get raucous from time to time. Back and forth. Rage for rage. The conversation would eventually become something like the old black church call-and-response. The call would come from the black person, and would be an expression of real anger, and why that anger existed. The response would come from the white person, who would say, "Jees, I never understood that you might feel that way. But, listen to what I feel about it." This was a very helpful revelation for both sorts of people in the groups. The Whites, who were almost all professionals, would have a black work partner or two who were also professionals, and who, the Whites understood, had clearly faced some kind of discrimination. But surely, they felt, those black people would not have suffered the kinds of anger and rage that a black man on the street participating in sit-ins and demonstrations, having come from Jim Crow, might routinely feel. For the Whites in our groups, coming to understand that rage was eye opening, and very helpful to what we were trying to get to. That is, that all black people are angry. That such anger is across the board with black people. Everyone."

Donnybrooks would then ensue, as will be seen.

In the last hours of these sessions, a dynamic of much deeper understanding would come from both Blacks and Whites. Blacks had let their true feelings be shown. Whites, too. Cobbs describes in a few phrases the changes he almost inevitably saw in every group he led. "When you're dealing that deeply in peoples' backgrounds, and things are uncovered on all sides, there has to be a period of cooling off and reflection. But at the end of every session…*every* session…no one…. It was very, very rare that anyone would be scapegoated. Things were sanguine. People had revealed so much of themselves to each other, that they now treated each other with real humanity, in ways that it deserved to be treated. There had been discovery, on both sides."

It has been many years since Price Cobbs led these kinds of groups. But he remembers with crystalline precision how he felt after every one of the sessions. "They were electric. Emotions had been raw. People standing up and bouncing around the room. People yelling. Someone else crying.

But there had been much more acknowledgment of what race and racism, the whole concepts of discrimination and prejudice, the practices of those things, really are. For both groups. The understanding on the part of Blacks of their own feelings of inferiority. Whites coming to understand how much a feeling of superiority—from birth—affected their thoughts and actions. It was all laid out for everyone to see. It was exciting. Sometimes dangerous-feeling, when an individual would get right up to the edge. And Blacks and Whites both would have understood how intertwined and inter-dependent each's actions and feelings are with the other's."

—

Pete Kranz came to understand all this from his own involvement with the two separate sessions, of two days each, that he attended, led by Price Cobbs and one of his associates, Ron Brown.

As Cobbs says, the opening session began with many initial questions, attempts to open people up, to introduce each other, etc. But Pete points out that, soon enough, the questions became more flinty and personal. What does each of you see as the primary issues of race in your own life? What did you grow up with regards to race? Did you know any Blacks? Cobbs asked of the Whites, and the same question reversed when put to black participants. What were the racial issues your parents had? Did they have hostile thoughts about the other race? Did your father and mother hate Blacks? Did they hate Whites? How did you feel about being black when you first encountered white people? What was the first thought that came to you as a white person when you first encountered black people? Where did those reactions come from in your upbringing? Etc.

Recalling this, a vibrant smile comes from Pete. "The room was small, and we were already sweating…together! I couldn't sleep that first night, because my turn was coming tomorrow, and I knew it was going to be painful…painful to explore my own prejudices in front of the group."

When asked what some of those personal prejudices are, Pete replies (to his white interviewer, the author of this book) immediately. "I have to tell *you*? If we're white, it's something we're taught for years. That black is bad. I don't need to tell you the specifics…white hats versus black hats. In a community like the one I grew up in…Jewish, itself suffering prejudice, with multi-cultural, thoughtful parents…that didn't happen. But outside, it's indirectly implied that white people must stay away from all that is not white.

"And after I talked about myself on that second day, people continued chiming right in, just like the day before…questions and answers about each other! How did one person at the table view some other person at the table? How did a black person at the table respond to me? What did his or her story or gestures tell you about how that person felt about me? This was a detailed series of questions, noisy ones, hurried ones, angry, humorous ones, one leading to the next, that required answers."

The questions had specific, direct intensity, and eventually would lead to real issues of race. One of the rules was that you had to answer. A shrugging of shoulders or a turning away from the conversation would provoke another direct question from Price or Ron.

"It was very powerful, this experience," Pete recalls. "We were all strangers to each other. Coming together, yes. But strangers! And Price and Ron really leaned on folks."

Ultimately the specific issue of racism proved to be vital, intense, and present in every participant's life, and neither Price nor Ron would relieve the pressure. The conversation had to go on, and participants were more or less required to react to what was being said, and to tell the truth—no matter what it might be—of their reactions. There was no mollycoddling. No one was let off the hook. Everyone had to take his or her assumptions about race, or about each other's assumptions about race, to their logical ends.

Pete describes it. "The subject material was so vital, so intense, so present in each of the participants' lives. And Price insisted on the truth in everyone's responses, no matter what the truth might be."

It is no wonder that these sessions were not peaceable, calm, or particularly kind. "Sure, there was often calm interaction," Pete says. "But there was a lot of anger. There was shouting, occasional tears, aggressive challenges, and sometimes hard-won understanding of views that may at first have been completely unacceptable to others around the table. But once we got to the understanding of why that particular person had that specific point of view…understanding would come even *then*, once the actual source of that opinion, from childhood, from parental brow-beating, from simple indifference to the problem, poor education, whatever…. So, the childhood of many of the participants was described. Your parents. The early schooling. Who else was in your class? If there were white kids around, how were they treated and, if there were black kids in the class, how were they treated? Schooling. Reading. Movies. Music. Your education. Your job. What are the things in all these issues or places that affect your views of the other race? What do you see in the other race that you love? What do you see that you hate? What do you see that you despise? The source of that opinion was being uncovered by the others in the session, and explained to the person who was voicing the opinion. Those were big moments of personal growth…for everyone."

In these confrontation groups, Cobbs and Grier often used a particular kind of seating arrangement. "There were two circles of chairs," Pete says, "one inside the other. A more or less equal number of participants were put in each of the circles. In terms of who was in which particular circle, the session leaders would configure it whichever way they wished. So…equal numbers of Blacks and Whites. Unequal numbers of Blacks and Whites. All black females. All white females. Black men and women all in the inner circle, white men and women all in the outer circle, or vice versa. Many configurations. The rule for each configuration was that those in the inner circle would then engage each other in conversation…or confrontation, depending upon the subject of the moment. The only requirement, which was an essential one, was that the subject of the conversation be something about race. Those sitting in the outer circle would be required to remain silent, and simply listen."

Price Cobbs describes the purpose of this seating arrangement. "This was the venue for the exploration of those 'eggshell conversations' that I felt were so much a part of the 'conversations about race.' Conversations I had seen so often, after some particularly difficult confrontation in the streets….riots, burnings, etc. Watts in 1965. Detroit in 1967. Etc. Those were earnest but overly respectable panels, discussion groups, independent investigations, etc., in which everyone was polite and discretion was the rule. The difference was that, in our confrontation circles, the egg shells would be broken quickly."

Dr. Cobbs wished the participants to discuss issues that they may well not have wanted to discuss. "We would often break the inner circle into two's and three's, and this proved to be a very effective way to get to the core of things." Indeed, the participants were frequently the ones who brought up the issues that would be discussed. Dr. Cobbs describes this phenomenon as coming from "motivation to get to things that hadn't been discussed or understood, from people who wanted them discussed and understood."

Splitting up into two's or three's offered the possibility that a given question could be addressed more or less intimately, between individuals. Very often, because of this closeness and the intimacy it offered, the sessions could become very difficult. Verbal exchanges were sometimes quite rough. There could be shouting, rage, profanity and often significant tears. "Yes," Dr. Cobbs says, "Breaking into smaller groups, even into individual pairs, opened the conversations in ways that a more general, larger-audience discussion would not necessarily have been able to do."

The arrangement also helped those participants who were either intimidated by the subject material or the possibility for real confrontation, or those who were simply very shy. "There weren't many of these," Dr. Cobbs says. "But I found that a gentle chiding with humor could bring such a person out, or a private conversation between me and that person during a break…. 'Gosh, Mary, I noticed that you didn't want to speak during that discussion this morning. Is there anything I can do to help you with that?'"

With all this, there was also often a need for a cooling-off period. When emotions were running very high, when one or more participants simply couldn't take it any longer, or if it seemed that a physical fight could indeed break out, the session leader would call a halt, tell everyone to stand up and shake it all off, and take the next fifteen minutes for a breather, for water, for the calming of emotions. "The leader had to pay attention," Pete says. "Things could get very intense."

Pete was already thinking about how he could use the experiences from these sessions in the implementation of such tactics in a class setting. "The Cobbs-Grier groups were very hard hitting," he says. "Confrontational, and often drawn out until Price and Bill felt that the individual(s) they were working on in the group had reached a certain racial understanding. I learned that I would have to temper how much I pushed someone, but that I would also *need* to push that person, in order to re-enforce his or her own growth. It was a fine balance that was achieved by Price and Bill, often under difficult conditions, and I realized even then that it would take a lot of energy from both me and my students, to achieve the kind of learning experience that I wanted for them."

Pete also describes the immediate aftermath of the two-day sessions he attended. "We were all together, and there was a kind of celebration. We had made it through! Food was brought in. The fact is that everyone… everyone!…felt connected, despite what we might have said to…or yelled at…one another." Pete nods as he reflects upon the aftermath of those celebrations and the two confrontation groups in which he had participated. "I was fired up!" He considered, with considerable self-searching, what he was seeing in the general population's attempts, or lack of same, to find solutions to the racial divide. Above all, after these sessions in San Francisco, Pete saw and understood the need for confrontation.

−4−

Bakersfield: The Idea-1

P ete returned to Bakersfield and work, and was soon asked to become involved in a situation in the Bakersfield public school system that featured racism and racial strife as its main elements. Communication between black and white students, teachers and staff members at South High School had effectively broken down. There were fights and confrontations on campus. Racial slurs and racist anger were becoming more and more of a problem every day.

To Pete, this was a systemic problem in all U.S. educational institutions. He felt that the growth of racism in schools was something that needed to be addressed across the board. "We had to come to terms with it, if we wished to live in a free world," he writes. "Racism has been fostered through fear, neglect, and ignorance, which have prevented educational leaders from placing it in its proper perspective and from instituting the changes needed to eradicate it. So the recognition of racism in all its seriousness is the first step to a possible solution."

Fresh from his involvement with Price Cobbs's confrontation groups, Pete felt he had some methods in hand for resolving the South High situation, methods that had never been employed by the school system, much less conceived of by it. He worked with Charles Siplin, who was a black man and the director of an organization called The Friendship House in Bakersfield, and had also been trained by Price Cobbs and Bill Grier in San Francisco. Sandra Nielsen, a white counselor at South High School, was the third member of the team, and central to its work. They approached the school district and the leadership of the mental health services with the idea of a racial confrontation group at the high school.

The very idea of doing this kind of thing in such a setting was revolutionary. It would be the first of its kind.

—

Pete describes the situation at South High. "Racial tensions had blocked any kind of adequate communication between black students, white students, teachers, and administrators alike. It was a disquieting disharmony, to say the least."

With Charles and Sandra, Pete went to the school counseling staff and the principal, and laid out a plan for a series of racial confrontation group sessions similar to those he and Charles had attended in San Francisco. There was, to be sure, one major difference between the participants in San Francisco and those that would take part in Bakersfield. This time, the participants would all be teenagers, none of whom was even slightly versed in the issues of psychology, psychiatry, social work, or any of the other fields from which the San Francisco groups had been chosen.

These were kids, not professionals.

With the principal's approval, and the basic requirement of oversight at every step of the way by the South High counseling staff and principal, the plan was put in place. Pete and his two associates began the process of choosing students for the group. After interviewing several and explaining to them what they had in mind, they named four white females, three black females, four black males, three white males, and one Asian male as participants. They also requested, and received, permission in writing for their participation from the parents of each of the chosen students. It should be pointed out that these fifteen students were not just "any" students. The criteria for choice were based on each's involvement in school activities, demonstrated leadership qualities, grade point average, and a basic level of interest in involvement with a group of this sort.

There would be ten sessions of ninety minutes each, once a week, held in one of the school's teachers' lounges. The lounge setting was chosen because of the level of comfort that could be found there, with soft chairs, couches, quiet, and a distinctly non-classroom feel.

All sessions would be led by Pete Kranz and Charles Siplin. Sandra Nielsen would also attend every session.

The two men had carefully spelled out between themselves their functions as group leaders. They were to provide a suitable environment in which the students could examine and express their innermost thoughts, feelings, attitudes and behaviors with regard to race. They were also to consider and discuss facilitating the sometimes unusual, untested, even experimental ideas offered by the students with regard to resolving the campus unrest. Informality was the rule. The students were encouraged to express themselves freely: their opinions of the racial issues at South High, their feelings about the situation, and their own prejudices. No cruel harassment of any kind would be allowed, no ridicule, and no physical attack. Respect for the individuality of each student participant was a must.

Finally, Pete, Charles, and Sandra were to meet every two weeks to discuss what they were learning from the students and how the students were reacting to the issues of race that were being raised.

Pete describes the initial few sessions of the racial confrontation group. "We spoke about the situation at the school, and gave a thorough introduction to what we would be trying to do with this group. But there was some question on the part of the students about what was really going to take place, a feeling of uneasy disquiet. Initial skepticism. Could a group like this really reach its intended goal, to resolve the racial tensions at South High?"

The skepticism came as no surprise to Pete and Charles. It was similar to that expressed by some of the participants in their San Francisco workshops with Price Cobbs, and in line with Price's own description of the way that the first hours of a confrontation group would find the participants trying to feel each other out, to knock at the door, to politely see what was possible.

Pete describes the anxiety and uncertainty among the students at South High. "The beginning session saw participants testing one another…superficially. They didn't want to start right off with probing or direct confrontations. The kids seemed to interact with each other more on an intellectual level than on an emotional one. So the students who more effectively could vocalize ideas tended to dominate these few early sessions. We knew that, during this stage, intellectual chitchat was normal to such confrontation groups. But we also knew that, as proper and careful as it was, this quiet intellectualism was blocking any evolving gut-level intense confrontation. It allows the individual to set up easy defenses to protect himself from facing his racial feelings. Involvement that required pure feeling was waiting in the wings, and we knew that."

Friendship was also an initial difficulty. Most of the students knew each other from their daily school activities, and considered themselves friends. "So, having a discussion in which there could possibly be a strain upon the friendship or the risk of actually losing it was a problem. For high school kids, keeping one's friendships intact, without question, is a major issue, even if the friendship is based on nothing more than the passage of a few words now and then on campus. So, the maintenance of that important relationship served to a degree to repress any direct verbal encounter that could threaten it."

Pete and Charles sensed, though, that that resistance could be dealt with if they stuck to their initial intentions for the group. "A supportive environment," Pete says. "Meaningful dialogue. A search for that dialogue and a determination to bring it to the surface." The two men calmly persisted with probing questions, waiting for those moments in which the actual racial issues would make an appearance. "We wanted the students to relate to each other on a personal level, in the here and now".

Something was indeed happening. Pete and Charles heard from some of the students in the group that, after their sessions together, they were having trouble re-adjusting to the normal classroom environment. It was difficult for them to concentrate on their regular classes, especially when (as we will see) the confrontation group brought more and more highly charged emotional reactions from the students. This too was to be expected, Pete and Charles knew.

From about the third session on, the atmosphere began changing. Initial defenses on the part of the students weakened. They started talking about their feelings, and taking the risk of being more assertive in what was a recognizable struggle on the part of each student to deal with his or her own racism. Pete recognized that the students were questioning their own "racial personas," as he puts it, and that previously protected inner suspicions, worries, and feelings about the other race were coming to the surface.

"Self-searching," he says. "And it was not a comfortable process." Discomfort or no, once these underlying feelings appeared in a particular student's reactions, the co-leaders and the others in the group would question the student more rigorously. "We didn't want that student to get away," he says. "Charles or me, and particularly the other students. We wanted to keep that person on the spot, and every student had his or her moment in that position."

At this point in the proceedings, raised voices were more frequent, and strong emotional outbursts became part of the norm.

"This is an important change for everyone," Pete says, "and the co-leaders need to remember a few quite vital things when it happens. We have to insure that empathic concern on the part of everyone is the ultimate rule. At the same moment, we want everyone to feel free to be as open as they wish, and willing to engage in real self-exploration on the part of the person being questioned as well as that of the questioners. And, of course, we want to insure the self-protection of the individual."

Maintaining respect for all three of these elements at the same time, during moments of quite heated back and forth in the conversation, requires significant calm and determination from everyone involved. It is not easy for the co-leaders; nor is it for the group participants. It represents, however, the opening of the door to significant exploration of the racial divide and understanding of the emotional damage that that divide does to each individual.

It was here that the real confrontations took place.

Ultimately, in the last few sessions of the confrontation group, the students discovered something for which Pete, Charles, and Sandra had been waiting. Openness was now *de rigueur*, while compassion for each other fueled the ongoing talk. Because of the insistence on emotional honesty and direct confrontation, the group began to understand that they were making a commitment to real action that could result in real racial change.

One student assessed the experience this way: "We started out completely white with white and black with black. But eventually I saw a change, a reaching out, and we began seeing each other for real: seeing each of us on the good and the bad, and finding out that we all had our 'hang-ups,' and then setting out to do something about them."

Another student took the experience a step further, and wrote something about it that would be re-stated in many different ways by others who were to undergo the process in following years. "The most striking thing that came out of the sessions was this: no matter what our problems or differences were, they were all part of a human experience...variations of [different] themes: pain, joy, suffering, just living day-to-day...all this."

A third student described finding real friends "who can talk honestly with each other about how they feel and believe, without fearing their 'being put down.' Friends who can argue and still care about each other."

Regarding the actual racial situation at South High, one may justly ask, "Did this confrontation group succeed in eliminating the problem of campus unrest?" The answer is a highly qualified "to some degree." Resolving the entire situation would probably require such confrontation groups among all the students at the school. Pete himself says, "Neither bigotry nor prejudice was completely eliminated. However, there was positive movement toward the lessening of past racial attitudes, beliefs, and actual prejudice."

What did succeed was the recognition of newly developed attitudes toward race on the part of the students involved in the confrontation group. These were real. All the students acknowledged them. They led to a formal understanding on Pete Kranz's part that the kind of learning he had received and the group he, Charles, and Sandra had formed at South High because of that learning, were key to a much larger undertaking.

$-5-$

JACKSONVILLE: THE IDEA-2

"I didn't know a thing about Jacksonville."

—Dr. Peter Kranz

The next year, 1972, Pete was named to a position in the department of Psychology at a new institution, the University of North Florida, in Jacksonville. He was a complete newcomer. "I only knew that I had been given the position. I was not aware of Jacksonville's racial history until I started teaching there and living in the community. But I quickly came to realize that Jacksonville was a city in the Deep South that had gone through terrific racial turmoil in the 1960s. Ax Handle Saturday and all the rest. I also realized pretty quickly that this struggle was still going on in 1972. Housing in the community was still segregated. And look at where they put the university! It necessitated a long drive from home for black students… if they had a car. I was sure that the idea I had for a class on racial confrontation would touch a raw nerve with many in Jacksonville. So, to tell the truth, I was lucky!"

When Pete arrived in Jacksonville that summer, he had no expectations that what he had established in Bakersfield could be part of a curriculum at UNF. But early on he discovered that a special program had been set up by the university, to encourage innovative ideas in education that may not fit very well into the usual mix of university courses and curricula. It had the name "Venture Studies Program."

The word "venture" is a tantalizing one, implying the presence of experimentation and creativity in whatever the undertaking may be. Two of the many questions Pete had when he first found out about the Venture Studies Program were "How experimental?" and "How creative?"

He learned that the program was intended for non-majors, and that innovative ideas, contemporary issues, and especially the possibilities for challenging the attitudes and behaviors of the students involved, were specifically intended by the university. So…there were courses in human sexuality, womanhood in modern society, bio-ethics, "the right to exist," and many others. These were issues that few colleges or universities even considered in the early 1970s. It was clear that the Venture Studies Program's offerings would be a major departure from the more normal rigors of "An Introduction to English Literature" or "Beginning Chemistry."

The knowledge Pete had gained at South High School was fresh in his mind, but he realized that he was now in the Deep South, where the political framework and social make-up were quite intensely different than would be found in California…even rural California, as was still exemplified by the city of Bakersfield in 1971. Jim Crow remained the legal framework for every state in the South. That system of prejudicial laws had suffered some significant reductions in influence at the behest of the federal government and the Supreme Court. But "States' rights!" was still a rallying cry for most southern politicians and state governments, and those "rights" served to maintain the robust health of statutes that discriminated against black people. So, Pete worried that any suggested curriculum at UNF that would actively feature racial confrontation would probably be frowned upon by the administration.

"But where I came from? And what I had learned in San Francisco and at South High?" he says. "I thought I should give it a try."

—

Here following is a description of the general situation in Jacksonville in 1972, from the point of view of one of the students Pete was to have, a young white woman named Judi, recently divorced with one child, who had grown up in Jacksonville. In 1972, she was twenty-five years old. She wrote this description some years after having received her degrees and raised her son.

"A younger generation, or anyone who did not grow up in the harshly segregated South, might find it difficult to fully appreciate the boldness of this venture. Most of us Whites had never had personal contact with a black person, just as most Blacks had not had personal contact with Whites.

"The University of North Florida was the first time I had been in an integrated situation. Blacks still rode in the backs of the buses, and were still banned from some other forms of transport. The news was still segregated, there being a white newspaper and a black newspaper. The news was reported, or omitted, accordingly.

"That we were kept separate, but by no means equal, made the idea for this particular course all the more startling in the early Seventies in the South. Indeed, it was amazing that the university even allowed the teaching of this class, much less actively supported it. Especially with risky experiential components like the home visit. Nothing like this had ever been done before.

"Now, in this class, we were a mixed group who would be exploring racial prejudices and our attitudes toward each other. This was not designed as an intellectual exercise. History would come into the conversation. There were books and handouts to read. But no tests. No term papers. Just a daily journal of our thoughts, feelings and experiences, as well as responses to written material, films, speakers, fellow classmates, and our professor. Active and honest participation was required, if not demanded. Pete promised that he would push and dig to get our 'gut feelings' out in the open.

"In our class, we found that all of us were having many of the same apprehensions. Some of us simply didn't want our routines interrupted. We were juggling work, school, spouses, and children."

—

Pete followed the protocols established by the university for outlining a course in the Venture Studies Program. There were many details, descriptions of process, philosophical explanations and so on, and the composition of his proposal was no easy endeavor. Also, he realized that it would have to pass muster with the chair of Pete's own academic department at UNF, the dean of Arts and Sciences, and the university's academic vice president. Here following are the salient details of Pete's proposal for a class called "Human Conflict: Black and White":

- Each class will have no more than twelve students, and will be race- and gender-balanced as much as possible, in order to promote diversity and open dialogue.
- Class sessions will be spent in discussion among the students, monitored by the instructor, on their attitudes toward each other's racial identity. Freedom of expression will be actively encouraged without the restrictions of political correctness. This will probably result in sessions becoming quite heated, with vulgar or profane racially charged expressions and language vigorously exchanged, if not shouted out. Because of the students' sensitivity, the depth of their emotional involvement in the issues of race, and the possible volatility of such conversations, the instructor must be a licensed clinical psychologist with training and experience in conducting group discussions of race relations.
- Physical attack will not be allowed.
- During the semester, each student will spend seven days and nights in a home of the other race. So, a white student in a black home, and vice versa. Students are expected to enter into dialogue with the host family and to participate in all daily activities. Married students with children are encouraged to bring their families, if the host family is agreeable to the arrangement.
- The class will make a weekend visit to a historically black institution of higher education. The purpose of this will be to give white students the sense of what it is like to be always a member of an ethnic minority. Also, black students will learn how it is being a member of the majority. The belief is that such a role reversal will sensitize both groups acutely to the feelings and perceptions associated with minority/majority status.

- A class reading-list will consist of ideological philosophies from black and white points of view. Required reading will include *The Autobiography of Malcolm X* (Malcolm X, 1966), *Black Like Me* (John Howard Griffin, 1961), *Confessions of A White Racist* (Larry L. King, 1971), *Black Rage* (William H. Grier and Price M. Cobbs, 1968) and other relevant titles of fiction and non-fiction. The reading will be part of the class discussions.
- Students are to keep a personal journal of their observations about the class. Though not graded, these journals will be collected and reviewed periodically by the instructor, who will make margin notes and comments to encourage further introspection concerning racial feelings, experiences, and attitudes.
- Occasional guests will join the class, from both races. Such speakers will represent diverse racial, political and ideological points of view. Guests may also be representatives of very extreme ideologies, such as those of the Black Muslims and the right wing nationalist White Citizens Council.

Pete himself describes what he was looking for in the class. "I wanted to teach a course that went beyond just lecturing. I wanted students to jump in and really get involved. I needed to get them to do more than just talk. I wanted them to feel...and to feel deeply. The only way to do that was to make the course experiential in nature. Talk. Gestures. Intensity. I had no idea what would happen.

"The dialogue and interchange among the students, with their looking at their own inner prejudices...Whites and Blacks...were most important. So the class had to be active, at times confrontational, while at the same time honest and accepting of individual differences. I told students to interact honestly and to talk in their own voice, in their vernacular, to say how they felt. The goal was greater awareness of racial differences, where before there had been little awareness or none.

"I was hell-bent to make a difference with this class and, by doing so, I was going to push the usual academic structure beyond its limits. I was not worried about what would happen if the class failed. The effort was worth the risk."

When the day came for the university's decision about whether to allow a course like this, Pete did suffer the anxiety that his idea would be rejected without question. Because the course dealt with extremely sensitive race relations, and included experimental components off university grounds during a time of high racial tension in the South, he knew it was getting close attention from the university administration. He fully expected to be turned down flat.

But the idea was approved. Support came from faculty, students and the administration; a kind of overall green light to the course. Pete Kranz immediately began his planning of the first class, which would be offered at UNF in the fall semester of 1972.

–6–

AN ARENA OF TRUTH

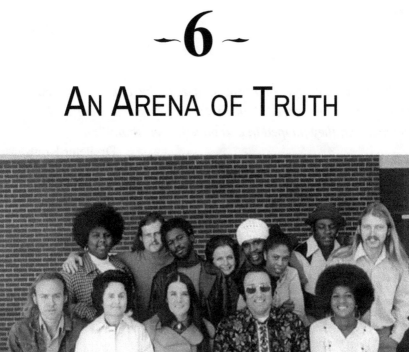

"I listened to comments from several of the white students, about how they relate to Blacks, and I could not help feeling angry. Why do Whites feel that the only way is the white way?"

         —a black female student.

"The class became an orgy of shouting, cursing, and intolerant discourtesy."

—a white male student.

"Without the courage of those students, the class would have failed. Some were scared. Some were angry. Some were curious. But whatever, they jumped in and gave it everything."

—Dr. Peter Kranz

THE JOURNAL

"I'm sorry for how I write, but my pen can't keep up with my thoughts,"

—a white male student.

O ne of the essential foundations for this book is the collection of journals that students kept during the period of Pete Kranz's UNF classes. Altogether, over the six years of the class's existence, approximately one hundred-twenty students participated, and forty-three of their journals still exist. Most of the personal daily observations recorded in this book from that time are taken from those journals, which the author has edited for grammatical consistency and basic flow, leaving all the occurrences, ideas, feelings, and philosophies intact for the perusal of readers.

A requirement of the class was that each student carefully keep such a record. It was the only significant written assignment the students had. Journals were written in privately, at various times of the day and night, in the library, at home, in a café…. Some were written in spiral bound notebooks. Others are loose leaf, held in order by a paper clip. These many years later, the ink has lightened in the journals, some close to fading. The paper clips are rusty. Those written in pencil are better off, and more readily readable. A few of the journals were typed, and you can still feel the rough indentations of the individual letters in the onionskin paper, even as the paper itself has browned or become stained. Of course, there were no computers then; so all the journals are actual objects. They have feel to them. They weigh something. In the writing, there is considerable unedited immediacy. Misspellings abound, and grammatical errors are frequent. Most of the writing is first-draft raw.

But these journals are also gems of specificity with regard to the daily issues in each class session and, especially, to the very felt emotions engendered in the students by each session. Cary, a white student, defined his reliance on the journal most succinctly: "I now know the worth of this diary. It's like having your own personal psychiatrist at your fingertips."

The journals give credence to the claims many decades later by so many of the former students interviewed that, while in the early 1970s, UNF's newness and its variety of courses meant something special to them, the class titled "Human Conflict: Black and White" was memorable...every session. They remember almost everything about the class in detail.

—

THE CLASS

"Here we are in a university classroom, facing each other, encouraged to look each other in the eye and tell the truth...how we feel about the others as a race. A lot of history has kept us apart. And that same history has brought us right here."

—a white female student

The first question in the minds of many of the students was, "Who is this Peter Kranz?" Pete was unknown on campus, a first-year professor in a brand-new educational institution. One of the students describes her first impression of Pete, on the first day of the new semester. "This man in his early thirties walked into the classroom with a book held under one arm like a football. 'Hello, I'm Pete.' Neatly dressed. Shirt and Levi's. Dark glasses. He was impatient and restless, exuding energy mingled with aloofness. Some of us thought he was a student himself because of his immediate close association with the others waiting in the classroom."

Another student writes about him, "He's Jewish and a Northerner, and perhaps is not even aware of the prejudice he will face from die-hard Southerners who display the Confederate flag with pride. This person is unfamiliar with this part of America, doesn't know the faculty or the students, and doesn't know how the students will react to one another in class. It's a given that things could become volatile or even violent."

Yet another says of Pete, "He describes himself as a loner. But I often see him in a group, gesturing broadly with his hands like the conductor of a symphony. He is impatient and restless, and exudes energy mingled with aloofness. People wonder who he is."

Pete himself assesses the situation thusly: "Some thought I was a little crazy, and that was why I thought I could get away with it. I may have been over-reaching, but I was young, cocky, determined, and focused, and I thought I could do it. I wanted the students to be able to challenge their own stereotypes, biases, and prejudices, through direct contact with the other group." Now in his seventies, Pete still moves about in his chair with restless excitability. These matters matter to him still, as much as they did in 1972. He removes his glasses, holding them in the fingers of one hand as he leans forward over his desk. A grin appears, and then a shrug. "I had to be the one to do the job." Both disappear as he lays the glasses on the desktop and considers his next words. "I felt it was about time that white folks got off their comfortable behinds and become involved, and aware of what was going on." A frown appears, but not one of unhappiness or defeat. It is rather an indication of what Pete realized at the time was one of the risks of what he wished to do. "The leader of these kinds of groups can become the focal point for hostility, especially from Whites. Whites have to go through the pain of racial growth and, naturally, as they struggle through it, they'll take it out on their white leader." Another shrug, equally confident, appears. "It's tough to be a bastard. But it's necessary. And as people go through the process that we'd all developed… Price Cobbs, Bill Grier, me, Charles, Sandra and all the others we worked with…a closeness is engendered, which comes directly from having to confront each other on personal racial feelings. For the most part, everyone involved ends up really caring for each other."

On the first day of each semester's class, Pete would settle himself into a chair and introduce himself. He then, immediately, would ask his first question of the day, of each individual student. It was the question that was to become the most remembered by all the students.

"Why did you sign up for this class?"

—

Ann, a black woman, began writing in her journal after the very first session. Her entry is invaluable because it gives the reader precise thumbnail sketches of each of the students in her class. Hers is the only description of a class's full complement of students to be found in any of the journals. She specifies that she is writing in light of the students' varied answers to that first question from Pete Kranz.

- "Mike 1 (white): Believes in white supremacy. Doesn't like Blacks in the white world labeling anything as their own. Angry because Blacks want to be equal.
- "Mike 2 (black): Overcompensates for the black cause. Feels that association with Blacks is the 'in thing;' therefore he wants in. Is willing to take risks on an intellectual level, but has fears on a very personal level.
- "Camille (white): Intellectually ready for integration on the professional level, but not so deep inside. Wants to understand why Blacks act up the way they do, but not to see how she could help fight for the cause of dignity for all people.
- "Harold (black): A middle-class pro-black with mild militant tendencies, but lacks the necessary tools to take a true stand. Opinions influenced by the "Hate Whitey" political environment, although none of them are based on actual experience with Whites.
- "Clifford (black): Middle–of-the-roader. Does not want to upset the apple cart for either race. Probably could be persuaded in either direction.

- "Judi (white): Typical white woman. Feels and lives white supremacy. Deeply embedded beliefs about Blacks. Fighting herself with what is right vs. what she was taught to be right.
- "Phillip (black): Likes being a 'token' Black. Has a feeling of superiority where most Blacks are concerned, and likes the idea of being a minority in the company of Whites. He has begun judging himself according to the white man's standards. Uses being black to compensate for other shortcomings.
- "Pam (white): Lacks complete understanding, but understands that there do exist prejudices. Does not know where to begin or how to look at Blacks for what they really are.
- "Pat (black): Typical black man in white society. Would be satisfied with getting 'a piece of the pie,' and not necessarily having to share it. Maybe caused by struggle and hardship. Wants to project the image of the 'good' Black. If not careful, could become white-oriented. Is seeking prestige.
- "Ann (myself): Pro-Black."

Ann's own expectations for the Human Conflict class when she walked into it that first day seemed dashed, right away. "I thought I must be in the wrong place. Some of the students didn't seem to me to have the kind of sharp intensity that a genuine discussion of race would probably require. Some of them were just too laid back, too lackadaisical. And when Dr. Kranz asked the question, 'Why did you sign up for this class?' the reasons given by the white students were for me beside the point, as though they were out to prove that they were willing to endure Blacks beyond the required situations and circumstances of regular college life. I also got the feeling that some of them were in the class in order to justify their feelings about Blacks, more so than to change those feelings."

—

The reactions of students to that first question from Pete vary. Here following is a brief selection of responses, as recorded in their journals by the students of various semesters during the six-year life of the class:

From Alfonso, a black man: "The first day of this class, I was a little disappointed because I had pictured the instructor as being black. After hearing the requirements for the class, and especially that first question, I was left wondering, 'What is this white guy up to?'"

From Cynthia, a white woman: "Wow! Jacksonville and UNF aren't ready for Dr. Kranz. But it's about time they got ready! I feel that I'm not ready for him either."

From Lee, a white woman: "I felt very ill at ease in the first class meeting, especially when I was interrogated about my feelings [about Blacks], as if it were my fault that I feel the way I do. I am a product of my upbringing, even though I know I reflect attitudes toward Blacks that are learned attitudes. For example, I have always had trouble distinguishing one Black from another. This must stem from my upbringing, when I never looked at a black person. They were just the help...the non-people."

Luther, a black man, entered class on his first day with a real set of nerves. He did not know what to expect. "I thought of copping out altogether," he wrote. "I wasn't sure I could handle it." Pete's question further alarmed him. "None of the dealings I've had with Whites in the past ever required me to give this much of myself. I've never been, or wanted to be, this close in my issues with Whites." Luther did stay on, however, and his unusual home visit with a married white man named Edward is described later in this chapter.

From Ann: "It's the segregation of races here [at UNF]. There is a very distinct grouping on this campus." Ann laments this, and then turns to her own involvement, or lack of it, in the racial separation she has described. "But I'm not back in school to socialize. Instead, I want to get my degree and to get out. But I do wonder if this isn't a cop-out on my part. Do I really feel this way, or is it just convenient for me to do so? And then, as I listened to comments from several of the white students in the class, about how they relate to Blacks, I could not help feeling angry. I could not for the life of me understand why myths have been allowed to survive for so long without more people trying to search for the truth. I wanted really to stand up and 'tell it like it is,' and especially to tell what it should be. But nonetheless, I felt drawn to this group [of Blacks and Whites both] that clearly had some sort of purpose. Although the purpose was not yet clearly defined for me, I still got the feeling that we were working toward some goal."

From Jack, a white man: "I was called upon in class to give my opinion regarding race relations. My references to 'colored people' and 'Negroes,' (habitual for someone of my age, fifty-four) instead of using the preferred term 'Blacks' seemed to mark me as more prejudiced than I had thought. Carlton, one of the younger black students, referred to me as 'the last of the Civil War veterans.' My speaking of youngsters as either 'boys' or 'girls' was not intended in the way that it was taken by some in the class. But I wonder if I'm deluding myself when I claim to be relatively free of bias."

On that first day, Michael D., a white man, had a nickname for Pete ("Krazy Kranz!") that he confided only to his journal.

From Cary, a white man: "Dr. Kranz asked me how I feel about Blacks. I said 'My generation of Whites is being punished for wrongs done to Blacks by our ancestors. But in general, Blacks piss me off. I feel they expect and demand a free ride.'"

June, a black woman: "I felt relieved. I had been carrying a burden, and never realized it. I explained my anger to the class, and right away felt more at ease with white people. It was my secret desire to express my anger to a group of Whites."

Patricia, a black woman: "The only Whites I noticed today were those passing by in their cars. If it weren't for this class, they would have passed me by without my even seeing them."

After that first day, Rex, a black man, spoke about Pete to a black physician of his acquaintance who was a practicing surgeon. The physician responded, "If this Dr. Kranz thinks he's so heavy, why doesn't he give his position to a Black?" Rex continues: "We debated the issue, and I tried to explain how the class wouldn't be as effective with a black psychologist in charge, because white students would resent him, or say that he makes those points only because he's black." The surgeon replied, "We should search for that white man's weaknesses and work on them. We should take over." Rex confides to his journal that he feels it better to work together to right a wrong that is three hundred-fifty years old.

From Judi: "I'm struck by the honesty of so many students, even when it puts them in a bad light."

—

Judi had a succinct answer to Pete's question that first day, although it reveals more or less settled expectations for her own understanding of black people than were later to be revealed in class discussions.

"Like other Whites in the class, I thought that day that I had it all together and would show any racists in the group a thing or two, as well as demonstrate to the black sisters and brothers how hip I was. I used the word 'Blacks', instead of the more traditional 'Negroes' or 'Coloreds.' I never used the word 'Niggers,' in my own household or anywhere."

But just a few sentences later, Judi's journal reveals an inconsistency in her assessment of herself.

"I don't recall what I actually said in response [to Pete's question]. The simplest and most honest answer would have been, 'Because I need it.' But before we even got to anything like that, he asked each of us to talk about our feelings about the other race."

Immediately a feeling of defensiveness welled up in Judi, worry that something that she did not wish to be exposed to others was about to be revealed…and recorded. "We didn't know each other at all. And there we were, about to say some maybe hurtful things about Whites and Blacks, right in front of each other. And it became clear that Pete was even going to write it all down on the blackboard."

Embarrassment seized her.

"I was not ready to clarify or expand upon any of that in front of a group of strangers: black or white, men or women."

There was more to Judi's worry than the simple wish to be self-protective or polite. Pete's question was about to bring some facts to Judi's attention, of which she had never been aware. For Pete, this was a good thing. Indeed that was one of the purposes of the question itself, for all the students…the revelation of actual and often, to this moment, hidden…assumptions about the students and their day-to-day lives.

"Like a lot of Whites, I grew up with some notions about Blacks that I felt to be wrong," Judi writes. "But I've never been challenged about it. Many of the prejudices came from my parents; and I suspected that the black students would assume that these were my beliefs as well. For example, did I assume that, because no Blacks had attended my schools, they hadn't gone to school at all? Was it no wonder that they were less well educated than I was? Later on that first day I discovered (Imagine! Something I had never really thought about!) that they had their own schools, on another side of town. I would also learn that those schools were not equal to ours in terms of quality. They were supplied with poor materials, and taught in poor facilities. On that first day, I would discover how much we Whites were the source of the problem, having banned Blacks from any form of real education in the company of Whites for many decades."

So…Judi was not nearly as "hip" as she hoped she was when she walked through the door into the class's first session. Right away, she came to understand some important realities that she had never considered previously, simply because she had been misinformed…all her life thus far. "That first day was my introduction to these things, and so many others. Here we were now, in an integrated classroom. Pete told us about the home visit, and then about the visit to an all-black college, which were things I never would have considered before this. I told myself to take in each of these ideas one thing at a time, the way I handled many things that were very worrisome, like getting a tooth pulled. But then Pete told us that, at any time, we could drop the course. This idea did pass through my mind the moment he mentioned it. But UNF provides classes only for students at the junior or senior level. No freshmen or sophomores. (Note: That was to change in subsequent years, as the university expanded.) So we're mostly older students, and I want to get the degree and get on with my working life. So I'll stay [in Pete's class] because I need the credit, and this course still seems like an easy 'A,'"

Judi was also to encounter that day the principal difference in the general manners of expression between Whites and Blacks. "We Whites took baby steps that first day. Blacks in the class were much more bold. They didn't hold back or stand on ceremony, as some of the Whites did."

There was immediate abrasiveness between Blacks and Whites, brought on by Pete's insistence that truth-telling be the norm, no matter the pain or embarrassment to others it may cause. Judi spoke of it in a later interview. "It's a wonder some of us were even speaking to one another after that class. The ice *had* been broken, but I felt I was still walking on thin ice. My parents' views, for example, had been absolute, with no exceptions. Blacks were not to be mixed with or talked about in any real ways. I did debate and argue with my mother and father, but actually I had very little knowledge or personal experience myself with Blacks. My parents didn't either."

Judi was able to quell her confusion by the end of that first class session. She had a son who at the time was two years old, and as the class progressed and each student explained why he or she had signed up for it, her particular reason for being there became clear to her. "I want to be educated in matters of race and, with this knowledge, to break the chain of prejudice that's been handed down to me. I don't want to pass on to my own son all the mess that we've been living with."

A deep-seated worry in Judi's mind about the relationship between Blacks and Whites is revealed by her use of the word "mess." She also reveals something of her attitude toward herself, pointedly, an attitude that would fuel her participation in the class. "Maybe I hope that having gotten through the initial unpleasantness of inadvertently insulting each other's race, we can now be friends." She reveals in her journal that this wish to be friends—to be accepted—had been a common thread for her throughout her childhood and early adulthood. "What is it about me that so needs to please, to be accepted, to be liked by others?" But on this day, these particular "others" are black people, and, towards them, that need seems greater to Judi, "as if subconsciously I'm seeking forgiveness."

—

Usually the class would be seated in a single circle, the students choosing where in the circle they would sit, and next to whom. This allowed for the continuous flow of conversation, and made it easier for the students to talk with one another...or confront one another...without having to turn around in a seat or otherwise discomfit themselves, as they would if seated in the traditional arrangement of seats in rows. But, as Pete had found in his sessions with Price Cobbs, the simple circle didn't always work so well. Cliques formed, in which a few students would always wish to sit together in the circle. In order to break up this arrangement, which could result in warring camps rather than in moments of individual expression, Pete retained the right to break up those cliques if necessary. Nonetheless there were moments when even the simple circle, as arranged on a particular day by Pete, would result in such difficult moments of confrontation that some other solution had to be found. In such cases, Pete could make use of the double circle idea. In one particular instance, for example, the inner circle (that circle that was to do all the talking, while the outside circle would simply listen) was made up exclusively of the white students in the class. In another, the inner circle might be all Blacks. In yet another, the inner circle could be made up of students who were particularly angry with each other. Or students whom Pete determined were pussyfooting around the issue of the racial divide, or molly-coddling each other because of a fear of appearing too confrontational. The purpose of the inner circle was to allow an even sharper light to be cast upon the particular points of view being espoused by the individuals in that circle. Occasionally, the two circles would exchange seats with each other, and the new inner circle would be asked to take up the issues presented by the previous inner circle.

At first, many had difficulties with this seating arrangement. As one student writes in her journal, "It was never going to be a comfortable situation...and Pete saw to that. If a white group tended to cling together, he would mix up the seating. He was canny, putting us with those we had had the most trouble with or didn't particularly like, because as it turned out these conversations had as much to do with personalities as they did with color." Another student writes, "This class was never going to be just about black and white issues. Gender would come into it, as would politics, economics, religion, sex...all the tough areas of debate."

Now and then, no seating arrangement was successful. The one inviolable rule in the class was that actual physical attack would not be allowed. The confrontations occasionally became so difficult that such an attack would appear imminent, as the verbal back and forth became more and more heated. Pete would then call for a cooling off period. He would simply stop the conversation and suspend the class for however much time he felt would be necessary for the combativeness to be eased.

"Get up. Get a drink of water. Take a couple of minutes for yourself. Calm down. Think about what's just been happening, and why. Take a walk...and we'll start the conversation again in twenty minutes."

—

One day, Pete made a presentation that further fueled Ann's suspicions that the white people in the class were, at best, misinformed in their explanations of themselves. He led a discussion about the integration of Little Rock, Arkansas's public schools, particularly that of Central High. On September 4, 1957, nine black students were scheduled to begin classes at the high school, which, despite its being a public, tax-supported institution, had heretofore been reserved exclusively for white students.

If such an event can be immortalized, this one was, by a news photograph taken by Will Counts of the *Arkansas Democrat*. It shows one of the black students (they became known collectively as the Little Rock Nine) named Elizabeth Eckford, walking on a Little Rock street on a bright, sunny fall day. She is one month short of her sixteenth birthday. What would be normal for a student beginning her time at a new school (excitement at the expectation of new friends and interesting classes, social clubs, sporting events, and the idea that her life is about to change as she takes her first steps toward a higher order of education than what she has known) was not to be on that day for Miss Eckford, for a number of reasons. For one, when the photo was taken, she was walking *away* from the school, having been refused entrance to it by the Arkansas National Guard. Also, she is being pursued by a crowd of white students...boys and girls...who are clearly heckling her. Like the other girls in the picture, Miss Eckford is dressed conservatively and well. She wears a gleaming white blouse freshly ironed, a flowing skirt white at the top, with checks below, and a white belt. Her curly hair is cropped short, and she is wearing a pair of horn-rimmed sunglasses. She is the only person in the photo wearing such protective eye-ware. She holds a notebook or binder of some sort close, with her left arm. The fingers of her left hand clutch the edge of the binder tightly. It is clear that she will not allow it to be knocked away.

The possibility for that to happen is also clear. Reporters witnessing the event wrote down some of the shouts that were being leveled at Miss Eckford: "Lynch her!" "Nigger bitch!" "Go home, Nigger!" At one point, she glanced at an elderly white woman past whom she was walking, and that woman spat upon her.

Behind Miss Eckford , the white students are clearly enjoying their efforts to make her feel very uncomfortable, even to the point of physically threatening her. Her own resolute facial expression shows that she is very aware of the possible danger that this moment represents. One of the white students, fifteen year-old Hazel Bryan, is following Miss Eckford, right behind her. Miss Bryan is caught at the very moment of yelling something at Miss Eckford, and under no circumstances can it be mistaken for a pleasantry. Indeed, photographer Counts said later that the exact words Miss Bryan was shouting when he took the photo were "Go back to Africa!"

All the white students in the photo exhibit similar threatening anger. Miss Bryan is shouting at Miss Eckford, her mouth quite blaringly opened. The other three girls in the photo are also white, and are dressed with as much stylish care as is Miss Eckford herself. Two of them, on Miss Eckford's left, are staring at her intently. Another girl, on Miss Eckford's right, is also shouting, although not at the black girl herself. This student is carrying a few books in front of her, ready for class, her left hand holding the handle of a diminutive wicker purse. She's blonde.

There was to be further harassment of one sort or another for Miss Eckford as the semester continued. But nothing was quite like that first day, although she was quoted as saying after those initial events, "I especially enjoyed my History and English classes." Will Counts's photograph was voted unanimously by the Pulitzer Prize selection committee to be awarded the prize for that year. Sadly, it was disqualified because written accounts of the events at Central High had earlier been awarded Pulitzers, and fairness dictated that some other photograph be chosen. Forty years after the event, Counts arranged for a meeting between Elizabeth Eckford and Hazel Bryan, and the two women actually began what became a shaky friendship that lasted for some years until, for various reasons, it was broken off.

Counts's picture was one of the elements that influenced President Eisenhower's decision to send in federal troops to assist the integration of black students to Central High.

After Pete's class about the Little Rock Nine, Ann wrote in her journal, "I got the feeling that, from everything said today, this story moved the class more than anything else. I could only envision this poor girl, but I felt I was taking every step with her. I wondered if the Whites in class could really relate to that, and what sort of commitment they could have made themselves. I looked up at the class and almost resented every White there."

—

Ann's journal is compelling reading for a number of reasons. She does not hold back in her descriptions of the other students, and neither does she spare herself. Ann has the kind of personal self-regard that allows her to see what the advantages are of this kind of human conflict, even when she is unhappy with what is being exposed about herself. She writes at length about the troubles she has had and seen as a black woman, and she is free with her opinions about the other students in the class, as well as about their perceptions of her, as she interprets them.

For example, she records a conversation she had one day with her classmate Mike, a black man, about their upcoming home visits, as required of all students. Ann understands that finding people who are willing to put up a student for a full week in their home without any foreknowledge of that person (except that he/she is participating in this class) is a lot to ask. When Mike shakes his head in admiration of the fact that it must be difficult especially for Pete to find such willing participants, they agree how "there is constant 'buck passing'", as Ann puts it, among people being asked to accept someone from the opposite race into their home. A husband says yes, while his wife puts her foot down. Or vice-versa. Or one person says he'd be willing, but he doesn't think his children will be up to it, so he cannot say yes, even though he'd love to do it. Just can't be worked out. Wish we could. Etc. Or vice versa.

"I wanted to know, specifically, why," Ann writes.

She describes the double-circle seating arrangement in the class, and what she has learned from its close intensity for the students, especially the Whites. "There seems to always be an attempt on the part of Whites to justify their feelings, instead of understanding and then breaking down the hostilities and myths they've harbored for so many years."

She worries when the confrontation she wants in a class situation does not take place. "I constantly listened in class today to the Whites and Blacks discussing problems. For some reason I became angry at both races." This is a complaint, but Ann goes on to include herself as one of the culprits. "I feel that most of us are trying to keep the conversation on an impersonal basis, rather than to let it hit home where it should." She discusses a part of one conversation, in which a black classmate, Philip, has been complaining about how his family was cheated out of money that was intended to help with the treatment his father was receiving for some important emotional counseling. Philip had bemoaned his father's treatment at the hands of his white caregivers. "Philip's family's difficulty was one of those times when something should have 'hit home.' But for some strange reason, I couldn't sympathize with him. I continue asking myself, 'Why should he blame the white man exclusively for swindling his father, when his family didn't do their part in getting the necessary help for him?'

One of Ann's white classmates is named Camille, who uses the term "colored" exclusively when talking about black people. "I've been called 'colored' many, many times. But why does it upset me so much when Camille says it? I don't believe she wants to change, so whenever she opens her mouth [about what she wants from the class] I see everything she says as a lie. But also, I realize that Camille's mannerisms and looks are basically the same as another young white lady I know that I dislike with a passion. Could it be for this reason that I so dislike Camille?"

On another day, Ann reacts to remarks from some students, black and white, in response to one white male classmate who has displayed anger at the way black people are routinely treated in the South. "Everyone was out to say something to support his militant sounds, as though he was for sure in favor of the black cause. But he's white, and white is still right in this group."

Having read some of these descriptions, the reader may conclude that the Whites addressed their anger and frustration principally at Blacks, and vice-versa. That is not so. One of Ann's most glaring concerns in this class is herself. She frequently writes about her own shortcomings, and does so often with painful intensity. "I can feel the scars of blackness, but I cannot let them justify my underachieving in some areas. I can resent the 'white establishment' when I feel I have been denied opportunities to achieve because I am black. But I can also hate myself because I have not taken advantage of every opportunity afforded me." Now and then, Ann turns her sharp lookout for racism against black people. "I can resent black people even more when they poison the minds of our young Blacks with their own prejudices. I hate it when I see a young black child unable to cope with situations simply because he has been taught that he cannot make it in 'white society'...thus causing him not to even try."

Her ferocity is eventually tempered, though, by the compassion she feels even toward those for whom, initially, she may have had angry feelings. One of the other black students in Ann's class is Harold, whom she described on the first day as "a middle-class Pro-Black with mild militant tendencies, but lacks the necessary tools to take a true stand." After a few weeks together in the class, Ann writes in her journal about a breakthrough she and Harold have made together. "I can see the internal struggle he is having with himself. I told him that I see him as an above average, wealthy black youth, growing up being rejected by his black peers because of his financial advantages. So, in an effort to prove that indeed he is black, Harold has assumed a militant role. This attitude, in some ways, helps to cover up his true feelings of rejection."

—

Martha was a young white woman who came to UNF for classes a few days a week from her home near Macclenny, a town thirty miles west of downtown Jacksonville. She was unusual in the class because of the distance she had to travel to attend, and was kidded for coming from a locale that was considered by other students as basically redneck. One of her fellow white students in Pete's class, upon learning that she came from Macclenny, described the town as being "not a place; it is a condition." Asked for an explanation, he talked about the obvious racism that he felt the town had always represented to him, referring especially to the Ku Klux Klan's notable historical presence there. He also offered the suggestion that Macclenny would be better located across the border in Georgia. This was intended as a humorous gibe, since all the other students in the class that semester lived in urban Jacksonville itself, a place they considered more sophisticated than almost anywhere in southern Georgia.

Martha arrived in the Human Conflict class the first day with a panoply of worries and fears about what she would find there. Her parents, upon hearing of her signing up for the class, objected strenuously, her father offering the enigmatic analysis that he liked Negroes well enough, but that Blacks were an entirely different breed or race, and that they were not to be socialized with. She recalls how, as a teenager one night, she and a girlfriend were driving home from a party, and lost their way while passing through the black section of Macclenny. It was an overly warm evening, and the car windows were down. But as they became even more lost, Martha's friend hurriedly rolled her window up. "My God!" she said as they passed through one particularly busy intersection, "Lock your door, Martha. There are Niggers everywhere."

Because she lived in the strictly white section of town, Martha had never had a real relationship with anyone black. She had attended all-white public schools, and recalls a conversation with one of her ex-high school classmates and that classmate's mother in a Macclenny food market. When asked what she was doing now, Martha told about her registering at UNF and how happy she was to be furthering her education. The friend asked her about the classes she was going to take, and Martha gave a rundown of the English class, the Introduction to Business Marketing class, and so on, finally making a passing reference to a class called "Human Conflict: Black and White." Pressed for an explanation, Martha spelled out in a few sentences what she knew about the class, information she had gotten from the explanatory paragraph in the UNF catalog for that year. Martha was excited about it because this was something so obviously new. She couldn't wait to see what the class was going to be about.

Both Martha's friend and her mother were immediately shocked. The older woman especially disparaged Martha's plan. She explained, "Niggers have no morals." She continued with a list of certainties that, she felt, anyone with half a mind would pay attention to before consorting with any kind of black people. Black people had worms that crawled out at night. They had burr hair that would fall out all over the place. They were dirty. If Martha were to actually spend a night in a black household, they would come into her room and hurt her when she was asleep.

The university also came in for some rough criticism from this woman. Clearly they were a bunch of communists on the faculty there, teaching things like this racial confrontation business. Martha would be brainwashed. "If you were my daughter," she said, "I would lock you in your room and never let you stay with Niggers."

Martha's former classmate offered a more conciliatory message intended, Martha thought, to soften the edge of her mother's intransigent attitudes toward white people mixing with Blacks. "We still love you, Martha, and we have faith that you won't do it. But you know, if you go, we'll have to see how much you change." The girl hugged Martha, and said quite softly, "My God! You've already changed too much."

On that specific day in Macclenny, Martha's views on race had not really "changed" in any particular way except for her having enrolled in the class. "I never noticed Blacks," she says. "They were there, but I didn't see them." She describes in her journal how it was that, as far as black history was concerned, she lived in ignorance. "Along with millions of other people," she writes. "where racial problems are concerned, I've always listened to my parents and friends, and gone along with them. That is the way I was raised."

The atmosphere in the class, however, was to change Martha's understanding in a profound way. She does not describe in specific particulars the hurly-burly of the racial discussions she witnessed and in which she participated. But we understand the results of those conversations when we learn from Martha herself about the changes in her thinking.

She writes about one of the first tasks the class presented to her: to consider the fact that she is white, and that "whiteness" is a state of being that needs to be understood if racism is to be understood. "I've never thought about my 'whiteness,'" she writes. She explains that, yes, she was born white, always will be white, and, moreover, is happy about it. "I will not apologize for being white, nor will I pay for something for which my ancestors were responsible."

Martha was described one day in class by a black student named Rex as being "that woman from Macclenny." Rex himself had plans to become a lawyer and to represent black people in civil rights cases. Implicit in his description of Martha was Rex's certain belief that Macclenny was a center of vicious racism against Blacks. "I'm an individual," Martha writes. "With individual thoughts, feelings, and intelligence." It's clear from her journal that, indeed, those feelings have been quite hurt by Rex. Martha protests in her writing that, even as Rex charges everyone living in Macclenny with being racist anti-Black, it is equally unfair for a white person to say that all black people are aggressive black-power militants who want to punish Whites. She pleads, in the privacy of her thoughts, for a clear view from both sides. She is not just "that woman from Macclenny." "For God's sake, learn my name. I know yours."

Another student in Martha's class, a fifty-four year-old white man named Jack, witnessed the rough treatment that Martha was getting because of Macclenny. He mentions in his journal that, although he is white, he is also a musician and that, because of that, even *he* has come in for some difficult treatment by the citizens of Macclenny. "I was *expected* to be a little peculiar. Even so, the only thing that protected me from the viciousness to which this poor girl is exposed in class is that I am a grown white man."

Martha sought advice from Pete Kranz. She explained the situation to him, and he responded with the advice that, since Rex had so nailed her with what Pete called "the Macclenny syndrome," she had every right to nail Rex, and to force him to explain his own militancy, and in particular its "in your face" manner. If there were things in Martha's upbringing that were offensive to Rex, she had the right to grill him about his upbringing, in order to expose the nature of his aggressive, insulting behavior in class.

Her journal does reveal that Martha faced up to Rex in class. Sadly, she does not describe in any detail the nuances of that conversation, of her own aggressiveness, and Rex's reaction to it. There is no mention of the confrontation either in his journal. But later that day, Martha writes in her journal, "Dr. Kranz, I love you to death for straightening me out about the 'Macclenny syndrome.' After talking with you, I gained enough strength to tell Rex a thing or two."

As the class unfolds through the semester, the tone of Martha's journal entries, and especially her attitude toward what she is learning in the class, shifts and develops. Martha is being challenged by Rex and the other Blacks, and it is having its effect on her. "At lunch today," she writes a few weeks later, "with my mother, an older lady whom I hardly know came up and said she had heard I was going to spend a week with some Niggers. I said, 'No, I'll be staying with a black family.' She said she was glad she wasn't me, and I said I too was glad she wasn't.'"

Martha's parents had a friend in Macclenny named Harley (a white man, of course) whose daughter, Martha felt, might be attracted to a black man she had recently met. With the mere mention of that suspicion, Martha's father descended into rank anger. "Does (Harley) want me to take my shotgun over there to his house and kill this guy?" Martha fell into distraught sadness. Her father was an educated man, she felt, a teacher, who was in many other ways liberal-minded. For the first time in her life, she suspects that her father, whom she loves, may be unable to understand the problematic nature of his reaction to this one situation. Martha confesses to her journal that she is deeply hurt by her father's outburst, a hurt she says she cannot describe.

She did not, however, let the violence of that exchange quiet her wish to open up her father's mind. Because he was a teacher, and her mother a teacher's aid in a primary school, one evening Martha opened a dinnertime conversation with them about education. She wished to know her parents' opinions of integration in the public schools. Her father reacted right away with his thought that Blacks in the schools lower the level of education for Whites because Blacks are not as intelligent as Whites. "It isn't fair, Martha, to slow down Whites so that Blacks can catch up."

Martha had been reading in Pete's class about the racism implicit in the IQ tests of the day, a situation that made sense to her once it was explained that all IQ tests at that time were written by white people. The students had talked in class about the inherent bias in favor of Whites in these tests, given the obvious tilt in the questions that would favor knowledge and understanding of white activities, white attitudes, white values, white...everything. "Dad," Martha said, "we'd be as dumb-seeming of everything if what we were trying to do was all based on a black society's values and knowledge." She further suggested that she now understood that Whites had suppressed the education of Blacks since they were brought to America, the most notable examples of that being the institution of slavery itself, the passing of anti-education Jim Crow laws, and the 1896 Supreme Court decision in Plessy v. Ferguson in favor of "separate but equal" education for Blacks.

Martha's parents were surprised by these opinions from their daughter, and gave their opinion that she was being brainwashed in that class at UNF. Martha stood her ground, and told her parents that she felt she *had* been brainwashed, but by *them*.

She does not record the reaction of her parents to this remark. But she does admit that she felt she had crossed "a major barrier" by standing up to them.

Eventually Martha formed a close friendship in the class with a black woman named Patricia, who came originally from Chicago and was now a citizen of Jacksonville. Patricia had described her initial dislike for Martha in her journal, especially because of Martha's upbringing in Macclenny. But when they finally did become acquainted, and found that they liked each other, she asked Martha what it really was like, being "that woman from Macclenny." Martha gave her many details, ending with the now firmly held observation that she had spent her childhood in a state of "complete and forced segregation." To Martha's surprise, Patricia told her that it was hard for her to believe that Martha could so easily talk about this, especially with a black woman. When Martha then told Patricia about her conversation with her father about Harley, his daughter, and the idea of the shotgun, Patricia laughed. "Well, I almost married a white man, once," she said, and both women laughed, hugging. "I wonder what *my* father would have done."

Martha's change in attitude did not go in her favor with many white friends who had discouraged her from taking the class. Some of them started referring to her as a "Nigger lover." She also encountered resistance from some of the Blacks in class, who felt that she was being a hypocrite with her new ideas because, after all, she was still white and she was still from Macclenny. "Where do I go from here?" she asked herself in her journal. "I understand why Blacks may hate Whites for all we've done to them, and I'm doing what I can to make this known. But if Whites reject me for this...and they are!...and Blacks won't accept me...what do I do?"

The dilemma was to remain for Martha throughout most of the semester. Nonetheless, because of the often cantankerous experiences she went through in class and her efforts to understand the depth of the influence that her upbringing had on her, she eventually felt more authorized to speak about racism than she had ever felt...a subject of conversation that, before the class, had gone right past her. "Don't tell me about Blacks," she wrote in her journal, "until you know the truth. You don't know if your beliefs are based on truth...because you have not ever heard the truth."

—

It is true that when Patricia, who was black, first met Martha, she took an instant dislike to her. That Martha came from Macclenny identified her right away as a racist, no questions asked. And also, Martha was so...well, white! Blonde, young, too much of a smile, too much charm, and clearly unaware of much that had anything to do with being black, Martha was right away a kind of enemy for Patricia.

The threat deepened the day Patricia saw Martha walking on campus with their black classmate Carlton. She watched the conversation, which was spirited and contained a good deal of laughter. Disgruntled, Patricia took a moment to assess how she felt about herself. She had just finished reading *Black Rage* and had found its chapter titled "Achieving Womanhood" the most truthful and insightful explanation she had ever encountered, of how simply *being* black affected the self-image of so many black girls.

In that chapter, Drs. Cobbs and Grier describe, among many phenomena, one specific one with which almost every black girl must at some time contend: "The first measure of a child's worth is made by her mother, and if, as is the case with so many black people in America, that mother feels that she herself is a creature of little worth…this daughter, however valued and desired, represents [that mother's] scorned self. Thus the girl can be loved and valued only within a limited sphere, and can never be the flawless child because she is who she is and—inevitably linked to her black, depreciated mother—always seen to be lacking, deficient, and faulty in some way…. In addition, [the black girl] takes her place within a historical context, in which women like her have never been valued, have been viewed only as depreciated sexual objects who serve as the recipients of certain debased passions of men."

Patricia sympathized with the women described in *Black Rage*, especially with regard to different shades of skin color. In her journal, Patricia tells how she feels: "As far as black girls being made to believe they're ugly, I learned about that when I was in grade school. I'm dark, and it was thought that the darker black people were ugly and dishonest." As a girl, Patricia simply came to believe this distinction, and it directly affected how she felt about herself and what she understood about the people who had actually voiced such things to her when she was younger. "I knew prejudice from my own race before I knew it from the white race."

Interestingly, the progression of difficulties from mother to daughter that Drs. Cobbs and Grier describe did *not* occur between Patricia and her mother. "My mother knew what was happening," she writes. "She always reassured me that I wasn't ugly, and she always dressed me nicely, even when the family was having bad times."

But seeing Carlton and Martha walking together, and perhaps

exchanging a certain kind of affectionate repartee, bothered Patricia. Martha represented for her something that had been bothering her since her childhood. Black women had been slave women to Whites, and so, even with the disappearance of actual slavery one hundred years before, in contemporary America the memory of that was, for a black woman, a very real one. And there were ample contemporary examples of how a black woman still could be similarly treated. In one particular moment in class, Patricia described a conversation she had with a white man when she was fifteen years old. "This is something I've pushed back in my subconscious. I'd nearly forgotten about it. But, a bus driver gave me a dollar...one dollar!... wrapped in a note, and told me he had ten cents for me later. The guy was in his late fifties, and white." Asked what happened, Patricia said, "What do you think? I gave him his dollar and note back."

Added to that is the power of modern advertising, as she read about in *Black Rage*: "A certain amount of feminine narcissism must rest ultimately on real physical attractiveness, and such attractiveness is determined by the artificial standard each community selects. In this country, the standard is the blond, blue-eyed, white-skinned girl with regular features."

In the early 1970s, this was very much the case and, for Patricia, Martha represented the essential success that that marketing ideal had achieved. "It raised in me some of the poisons that we were talking about in class, and those poisons definitely run deeply," Patricia confides to her journal. "I have to get this attitude out on paper in order to deal with it. I'm tired of white women dominating the few men we have. There still are some of us that prefer black men. Only there's not enough [of them] to go around. As if we don't have enough competition, Martha has to put her 'lily white' two cents in! I don't hate you, Martha, but that particular time [seeing you with Carlton,] you represented the white women that I resent."

One can imagine Patricia resting her pen on the tabletop as she contemplates what she has just written...especially when she takes the pen up once more and continues writing. "I can't believe I finally came out with it. I finally realize what it is that I have against white women: black men! Now I can try to deal with it; but first I had to know what it is."

As she went through high school, Patricia had some very positive factors in her coming to understanding of herself. She had long hair that, among her young friends in school, was unusual. This alone gave her a kind of self-confidence because she so often was complimented for her hair. The other element...and one that Patricia knew was valid because she was so often given admiring credit for it...was her intelligence. She was smart, and very aware of it. Patricia read, especially in the literature of black history and black civilization in the United States. She describes in her journal the reaction she had to a conversation in a UNF history class about the differences between Henry David Thoreau's essay "Civil Disobedience" and Dr. Martin Luther King Jr.'s "Letter from the Birmingham Jail."

Published in 1849, "Civil Disobedience" is a landmark document in American writing. If Thoreau's famous book *Walden* is a song of praise for living in the woods, discovering the secrets and difficulties of nature, and seeking the keys to a satisfying spiritual life in solitude and the study of the surrounding world itself, his 1849 essay "Civil Disobedience" is a political tract in which Thoreau considers the obligation of the state to the individual and, more important, of the individual to the state. It remains to this day a radical challenge to the power of established governments, and as such it continues being the fiery call to individual political expression that it was when it was first written. "I heartily accept the motto,—'That government is best which governs least;' and I should like to see it acted up to more rapidly and systematically. Carried out, it finally amounts to this, which I also believe,—'That government is best which governs not at all;' and when men are prepared for it, that will be the kind of government which they will have. Government is at best but an expedient; but most governments are usually, and all governments are sometimes, inexpedient."

Dr. Martin Luther King Jr. wrote "Letter from Birmingham Jail" on April 16, 1963. He had been incarcerated for his planning of and participation in non-violent demonstrations against government and business segregation in the city of Birmingham, Alabama. Several other demonstrators were jailed with him. While in his cell, King received a letter from eight white Birmingham religious leaders, who agreed that social injustice clearly existed in the city, but that there was an established legal system, assisted by established courts of law, through which that injustice could be legally addressed. Illegal demonstrations in the street were not the way.

Dr. King addresses this early in his own letter. "My friends, I must say to you that we have not made a single gain in civil rights without determined legal and nonviolent pressure. Lamentably, it is an historical fact that privileged groups seldom give up their privileges voluntarily."

He makes clear that the call to wait has been made since the institution of slavery itself, and that significant actual change, especially in the organized and enforced segregation that still thrives in the southern states, has never come about.

Dr. King also addresses the concern of the white religious leaders that his involvement in the efforts in Birmingham are those of an "outside agitator." Such intrusion is unacceptable. How does someone based far away in Atlanta, Georgia feel it his duty to interfere in matters that strictly affect the citizens of Birmingham, Alabama?

"I am cognizant of the interrelatedness of all communities and states," King writes. "I cannot sit idly by in Atlanta and not be concerned about what happens in Birmingham. Injustice anywhere is a threat to justice everywhere. We are caught in an inescapable network of mutuality, tied in a single garment of destiny. Whatever affects one directly, affects all indirectly. Never again can we afford to live with the narrow, provincial 'outside agitator' idea. Anyone who lives inside the United States can never be considered an outsider anywhere within its bounds."

He also addresses the basic issue of breaking the law, by making a distinction between just and unjust laws. "Any law that uplifts human personality is just. Any law that degrades human personality is unjust. All segregation statutes are unjust because segregation distorts the soul and damages the personality. It gives the segregator a false sense of superiority and the segregated a false sense of inferiority."

In one quite long paragraph, King famously lists, with heartfelt power in his writing, the injustices visited upon black people. The paragraph begins with an actual, well-known, but nonetheless startling fact: "We have waited for more than 340 years for our constitutional and God given rights."

Patricia enjoyed both documents. However, another student in the history class in which she was enrolled, a white woman, found what she felt was a telling difference in the two men's lives at the time of their writing of the essays. Patricia describes that difference in her journal. "That white lady said, 'Yeah, King's letter is important…but King had to have a crowd of people to inspire him, whereas Thoreau only had Walden Pond.'" Patricia is offended by the white woman's finding fault with King's having supporters with him. She feels that the woman's observation has nothing to do with the quality and depth of King's ideas. Rather it belittles the conditions of his incarceration with so many others in the Birmingham jail, even as that incarceration is singularly unjust and is the very event that brought about his letter. "I tell you, that woman is so stupid. She tries to put down anything a black man has achieved," Patricia writes.

Eventually, Patricia was able to soften her resistance to her classmate Martha. The intensity of the talk in class, and its argumentative insistence upon truth-telling no matter what that truth might be, had the effect of forcing the students to consider ideas about each other that would never have surfaced otherwise. Patricia particularly wished to be honest with Martha about her earliest attitude toward the white woman, when they first had met. She had learned eventually that there was more sincerity and self-examination in Martha than her mere appearance may have suggested in the beginning.

In a moment alone toward the end of Martha's participation in the class, Patricia actually exposed her initial feelings toward Martha by showing Martha the entries to her journal in which Martha was specifically mentioned. These entries displayed distrust, jealousy, and anger. Patricia did this so that she could then tell Martha how profoundly her opinions had changed. It was the opening of Patricia's heart to her perceived enemy, and Martha understood that. Patricia writes, "I wanted her to know how I felt about her at the beginning of the class, and how I feel about her now. I feel I have a very special relationship with Martha, and I wanted to become real with her."

—

Carlton was a black student, in his early twenties when he was in Pete

Kranz's class. An avowed black nationalist, he was generally thought by the other students, black and white, to be the most outspoken and, as one student put it, "militaristic" of them all. He was indeed a veteran of the U.S. Army, and had served in Southeast Asia.

Carlton had attitude, and had little trouble voicing his rage. He wore sunglasses during most of the classes, dusk-like coins of darkness that allowed little indication of involvement or change in his attitude. You couldn't see Carlton's eyes. And, although quite outspoken, he also offered a very clear point of view when he was completely silent. Wordlessness seemed one of his tools for expressing anger. He looked down his nose at most of the students (Whites because they were the oppressor; Blacks because they were "Uncle Toms."), and when he did speak, his steady, downturned voice, a kind of weapon in its own right, convinced the others that Carlton hated being in the class, and thought that the others were fools.

Carlton's journal entries are few. But they have a direct eloquence and singular clarity of intention that are difficult to find in the other journals. Here is some of what he wrote at various times in his journal.

"Cultural differences are so great that most Blacks will avoid close-quarter confinement with Whites as much as possible. I spent a very pleasant evening with (my classmate) Rex. Personally I think he has achieved more growth and insight from this class than any of the other Blacks involved. Until the class started, this man was living in a state of illusion and fantasy concerning the racist nature of this country, whereas I have known of and confronted white bigotry for as long as I can remember. The class has only re-enforced my contention that 'Crackers are crazy.'"

"I don't consider myself fortunate or lucky to be a student at UNF. Everything that I've accomplished has been on my own merit. This society does not owe me a thing, and I definitely don't owe any debts to this society. I hate the system. The poor get poorer, and the rich get richer. The Whites die slower, and my black brothers die quicker."

"When I look closely at the international economic and social structures, the universal race issues, I have serious doubts about the Almighty's ability to right the wrongs created by white supremacists. Man, these crackers don't want to lose an inch of their so-called superiority. Like today, I spent most of the afternoon trying to console my girlfriend, who's white. Her landlady has finally shown her true cracker nature. Last night, the land-lady told my girlfriend she was headed for big trouble dating that Nigger. If it continued, she would have to go to some other residence. "

"I lived abroad for some time in a more racially harmonious environ-ment. So fucking what? I've fathered a hybrid child. I 'played' husband for an extended period with a couple of white ladies. So fucking what? None of that illuminates nor eliminates the racist nature of my daily existence here in 'Amerikkka' today."

"Pete, your class is a fucking drag sometimes. It seems to me that a lot of the methods you use at this state of our development are obsolete, outdated, and completely irrelevant. Sometimes the class is a journey to Utopia, where everybody functions in harmony with one another. At other times it sounds like an old-fashioned revival meeting where everyone con-fesses their sins and pleads for repentance. Other times it comes off like a criminal court room where the whole white race is on trial for raping the black race, with the judge, jury, and court officials all white. Verdict? Charges dismissed, while out here on the streets, the crackers are still act-ing up. This nation is doomed to rupture soon. I've asked Santa to bring me another shotgun for Christmas."

Carlton left the class on the last day of the semester, walking away in silence. He maintained a social connection with very few of his classmates, and those he did maintain were eventually abandoned. A conversation with him forty years or so after his participation in the class would perhaps re-veal great change of heart…or ever more militancy. But Carlton was gone, and that conversation could not be had.

—

Art was a white male Jacksonville policeman, married for some years when he took the class. As with Carlton, the style in which he expresses his views is unguarded and violent. To be sure, there is plenty of prejudice in most of the class journals and a good deal of real resentment, Blacks for Whites and Whites for Blacks. Art's is the only one extant in which a white student lays out in complete, unrestrained detail his deepest feelings about the other race. There are many reasons to read selections from his journal because, like Carlton, he is so unequivocally truthful about how he feels, even though that truthfulness is almost unremittingly acid. I present several portions of Art's journal here because it is so revealing of the white racism that still existed in the South (if not in the entire country) with such vehemence in 1972. It also shows convincingly the effect that the class is having on Art's thinking about race. Some of what he says about what he is learning in the class comes as a shock because it seems impossible that such a racist could ever turn from his own hatred of Blacks. The racial "understanding" that Art sometimes espouses could be simple confusion on his part, muddled thinking that he takes as revelation.

But it may actually *be* revelation.

Here following is a selection of entries from Art's journal.

"I found myself very apprehensive about this class. I kept telling myself I could bluff my way through it. Just 'hang in there' and the 'Niggers' won't get to you. I feel a little sorry that the black people have had such a hard time, but I don't feel I am responsible for the position they hold in America."

"I've been getting a lot of smart remarks from my friends. I've been told to 'snuggle up to mammy,' to be sure and 'tap' the sixteen year-old daughter, and to be careful not to 'come back a 'fudge-cicle.'"

"Inside my head are two little voices: one tells me to look at each Black I see as a person; and then the other jumps in and says, 'Don't kid yourself. Nothing is going to change. Blacks are all alike. They don't really want to change any more than you do.'"

"I rode in a patrol car last night through a predominantly black area. I wanted to find out what it was like for a white policeman patrolling a black area. I noticed that, as we passed, each black face stared directly at us until we were out of sight. Those stares told me the whole story: all the fear and hate in a thousand eyes trying to stare you out of existence."

"I just found out what is really bugging me: the quota system. Because I'm white, I now get excluded from certain loans, certain scholarships, and certain schools, in the name of 'racial balance.' It pisses me off to be the one who has to pay for the 'racial injustice' of the past two hundred years.

How can you help but have a certain amount of hate for reverse racism. The white middle class and poor American is being pushed aside, and he will become the 'black man' of tomorrow. His enemy will be the government."

"I want to avoid that guy Carlton in the class. I get the feeling that, underneath, he's laughing his ass off at a bunch of whiteys playing their white game in order to make the Nigger complacent. The shoe's on the other foot, and I don't like it. I understand how Blacks have built up such hatred; but a voice in me says 'Guard yourself because they're trying to put it all on you.' Maybe I'm responsible for the cure, but I don't feel responsible for the cause."

"My employer says everybody should 'own a Nigger.' My friends get on my back for talking to Calvin, the Nigger next door. I am struggling between wanting to change the way I relate to Blacks and wanting to keep the friends I have. There have been many times when I wanted to say to someone, 'Why do you call Blacks 'trash' and 'Niggers?' What have Blacks ever done to you besides wash your clothes and dishes?' But if I did, they would just laugh their asses off, and I would be laughing with them, to cover my own ass. I'm a phony."

"I thought *Black Rage* was a lot of bullshit. I tried passing it off as black America trying to blame everything on us Whites. But after talking to Calvin, I can see how white America has caused so many problems for Blacks. So many things working subtly against them."

"It's weeks now into the semester, and I've thought seriously about quitting the class. I can feel my wife and myself pulling apart in our thinking. It hasn't caused any serious problems yet; but I can see it heading that way. The class doesn't cover just Black-White; it covers all of life. How you feel about every other human being. And how we white Americans have gotten the notion that we have a right to the bigger slice of the pie. We've pushed aside the Indian; entrapped the Blacks; spat on Jews; ignored Cubans. Because they have different skin color and/or a separate language, and have customs we don't even try to understand. We have seen others put into detention centers because they are a certain race; watched others being killed for wanting to use a certain bathroom or for wanting as much from life as any White wants. We are a nation of dead minds and empty hearts."

"I've been surprised by most Blacks I've talked to about this class. I thought I would get as much flak from them about how useless the class is, as I've gotten from the Whites I've talked to about it. But most of those Blacks… in fact, *all* of them…think that it's great that something like this is happening."

"All civil service employees should be required to go through training programs such as this class. The police departments I'm familiar with are predominantly white. I've ridden with and listened to white racist cops, and know they are a big part of the problem. I've seen the white cop who couldn't have cared less if Blacks kill each other off, who thinks that Blacks are automatically criminals, who feels powerless in the black community unless he has his gun ready at all times. I've found out that the policy of this city is to arrest as many people as possible."

"Just before Thanksgiving, I drove fifteen hours to Kentucky. If you think things are bad in Florida, you ought to come to 'snow white' Kentucky. People there aren't subtle about their racial hatred. They run off at the mouth about the 'Niggers' in 'their' state all the time. I'm from lily-white America myself. But in Kentucky, most of the people I met were middle class or well-to-do Whites and, from what I saw, have a total hatred for Blacks. For the first time I have some idea of how it is that I am a racist. Racism can only destroy America…and there are a million walls out there, Dr.Kranz."

"I confess I am a racist. I confess the poison is deep. It's like being an alcoholic, who's always got to keep his guard up, or with only one drink he can get caught up in his sickness again. The sickness can't be controlled. I confess I've hurt inside and will hurt even more in the future. But the people in this class…you wanted me to see my responsibility. You wanted me to understand my gut feelings, You wanted me to open myself up. You pulled out my tears. You've had my hate. You've earned my respect. I've earned my respect."

TOUGH TALK

"My family felt that it was bad manners to use ugly words."
—a white female student

As with the sessions that Pete Kranz attended in San Francisco with Price

Cobbs and Bill Grier, those that he designed and led at UNF were often far from peaceful. Indeed they more often contained anger, forgiveness, weeping, shouting, accusation, pleas for understanding, profanity, name-calling, and tearful embrace than they did sanguine expressions of the wish for "a conversation about race." But these truly *were* such conversations, ones that had the desired effect of bringing about actual, unvarnished understanding of what Blacks feel about Whites, and vice versa. Those understandings, having been acknowledged, would lead, it was hoped, to direct action to eradicate the barriers that stand between the two races.

But the behaviors were risky. Hatred between the races was a reality, as had been proven by the previous three hundred fifty years of history in the United States. That history had resulted in positive legal changes for black people only during the period after 1863. But even in the time following the Emancipation Proclamation (signed that year) the efforts by Blacks to achieve equal rights (at least legal rights) with those of Whites faced very difficult opposition.

Jim Crow was the most vivid demonstration of that claim, as was the practice of lynching. During the 1930s, the act of lynching itself went into decline as a way favored by some southern Whites of getting rid of specific Blacks that they did not like, and of terrorizing the black population in general. But the justice systems in the Southern states continued to provide ample opportunity to execute black people, at a rate disproportionately greater among the prison population than the percentage of black people in the overall population. (Although lynching was less frequently a practice in the North, the prison population in those states still featured a black presence that was far beyond the percentage of Blacks in the general northern prison population.) In 1972, the U.S. Supreme Court heard the case Furman v. Georgia, and struck down Georgia's death penalty statute. The court found that that statute closely resembled "self-help, vigilante justice, and lynch law" and that "if any basis can be discerned for the selection of these few [individuals] to be sentenced to die, it is the constitutionally impermissible basis of race." Senator James O. Eastland of Mississippi, a white man, opined that the Supreme Court was inappropriately legislating, therefore "destroying our system of government." Georgia's Lieutenant Governor at the time, Lester Maddox, a white man, said that the decision provided a "license for anarchy, rape, and murder," and added, "There should be more hanging. Put more nooses on the gallows. We've got to make it safe on the street again.... It wouldn't be too bad to hang some on the court house square...."

This during the initial year of the Human Conflict class at the University of North Florida.

Risky behaviors or not, the students in the classes persisted in bringing their racial differences to the surface of their discussions, and airing them freely, no matter the consequences.

Following are brief examples of the kinds of conversations that were regularly held in the Human Conflict class throughout its history at UNF. They were put together from descriptions in class journals, interviews, and conversations the author has held with various students and home hosts. The author wishes to point out that there are very few actual, substantial exchanges of dialogue recorded verbatim in any of the student journals or subsequent interviews. Rather, students will describe what a conversation was about, the level of candor, friendliness, or anger between him/her and whomever was also involved, or the importance of what was revealed to the students in any such exchange. For the most part, these journal descriptions are written in plainspoken prose paragraphs. The eventual effect of the conversation upon the feelings of those involved is once again presented in prose paragraphs. The author hopes the reader will peruse what follows here with an open mind and an appreciation of his efforts to make the conversational exchanges as accurate and realistic as possible, given the circumstances.

—

We have read earlier in this book about the tendency of Whites in the class, at first, to hold back in their opening gambits about the racial divide, while in general the Blacks spoke out freely about it. One significant such conversation took place in a series of classes in 1972, and featured the voices of a fifty-four year-old white student named Jack (the same man who sympathized with Martha for being called "that woman from Macclenny"), and two black students, Ann and Carlton.

Jack kept his journal carefully, and opened his heart to it at length. He was unusual because of his age, the great majority of the students being at least two decades younger than he. He was born in "the South," he says, although he does not name the actual location or state. By the time of the class, he had lived in Jacksonville for almost fifty years, his parents having moved there when Jack was five. He served in the Navy as a medical corpsman at Parris Island, South Carolina, the famous training site for the U.S. Marine Corps.

From his many journal entries alone, the reader gets the feeling that Jack is a gentlemanly sort, a courteous man, and somewhat old-fashioned. He has had a working life in various fields, business and otherwise, and has come back to school because he wants training to be a school counselor. Despite his age and his generational distance from most of the other students, and his courteous wishes for mutual understanding, Jack was at the center of a cantankerous class dispute in which he was engaged principally by Ann and Carlton, who were much younger than he. He does not understand their behaviors, and is certain that they view him as the kind of passive white Southerner who has simply allowed racism and its attendant ills to continue to exist, without comment, for his entire life. He thinks this appraisal is an unfair one.

Other conflicts in the classes are being presented in this chapter, but this one has a feature that those between students of a similar age do not have. When we hear Ann and Carlton arguing with Jack, we hear the racial differences with which all three came to the class. But we also see evidence of the way that older, traditional Whites viewed Blacks. And we see how younger Blacks are not going to put up with the sort of manners and gentilities that have so hidden the real racism of so many Whites in the historic South, if not everywhere in the United States.

About five weeks into Jack's semester in the class, Pete Kranz invited a black woman psychologist (I'll call her Professor Smith) who was on the faculty at UNF, to sit in on a session, and the woman agreed. She entered the classroom in the company of an older black woman: Professor Smith's mother. Both were dressed carefully and well, and it was clear to everyone in the class that these women were educated and quite capable of active involvement in whatever conversation that may develop. Jack describes the situation at some length in his journal, and his assessment of the older of the two women is a clear indication of how he was raised and what his views were toward black people in general, and these two women in particular.

"The mother, Mrs. Smith, is a very feminine, intelligent, pretty black lady of apparent middle age. She has seven children, all of whom are successful and have evidently given her no real problems of behavior. Not that they are the docile type of Negro bending and bowing to the white race; rather they are successful in their own rights by virtue of their own efforts.

"I am reading *Black Rage* at this time, and the authors take great pains to explain the matriarchal type of family so prevalent among Blacks. Mrs. Smith did not give me an impression of being matriarchal; she seemed to me to be only a younger example or prototype of my own mother.

"Since she and I are of the same generation, I was interested in her answers to the many questions asked of her by the younger students, black and white, about her feelings regarding segregated water fountains, restrooms, and such. It seems that she, like myself, being products of our time, didn't normally give much thought to these things. We just accepted them as the way things were. Evidently what one is born into and lives with not too uncomfortably, does not hurt so badly as long as it is only what one expects of life anyway.

"I am sure that there are other forms of discrimination that did hurt Mrs. Smith, that she probably resented and even felt anger about. These would be things that I might not even have noticed or thought about, because I was not the victim. I have learned recently that there are many subtle forms of discrimination that many of us are completely unaware of, and she has probably purposely repressed these incidents.

"I was approached after class by a young white male student. He was also very much impressed by Mrs. Smith's gentleness, and remarked that he was glad she seemed so lacking in bitterness. He contrasted her remarks and her not unkindly feelings toward Whites with those made [by some of the young black students] after I stated early in the semester that I was myself quite unbiased about Blacks. My answer to him was that probably both races [during my youth] were fairly content with the status quo, and that it has taken the youngsters of this generation to drag us into the position of having to face up to the facts that we formerly found it convenient to ignore."

This is a measured, quietly stated description of Jack's understanding of the racial situation in the South, for his generation. It is also beside the point because it does not acknowledge—indeed has no apparent interest in—the possibility that Mrs. Smith might have a different opinion than the one he believes she has.

But Jack was not to be allowed to simply hold these views without having them contested.

Ann particularly criticized Jack that day for what she felt was his blasé attitude toward race relations. She took special offense when he said in class, "I haven't called an elderly negro 'Uncle' in several years. I don't suppose I ever will again. I feel a nostalgic sense of loss, though. I wonder if any of the old 'colored folks' would know how I feel." Ann shouted at Jack that he was a blatant white racist, even as he did not understand that about himself, and would deny such a charge. Ann felt this made his racism even worse because it was so blind to itself. He protested, asking for a more balanced and considerate view of how he felt about black people (respect for them, his lifelong kindness toward them, etc.), and Ann began what Jack, in his journal, described as "a verbal brawl."

"The class erupted," he writes. "Although maybe it was contrived, because Ann seemed to me to agitate and encourage the continuation of the arguments. Maybe this brings previously hidden feelings into the open, and consequently was purposely arranged. The shouting, arguing, interrupting, and refusing to allow anyone a chance to complete a statement or answer or direct a question did not really help me to understand."

Jack contrasts this session with the many previous ones in which he had participated. In his journal, he has congratulated the class for having "talked together and, even while criticizing, having attempted to learn to understand each other's racial prejudice." He has used such terms as "a gratifying experience," and "developing friendships" to describe the class so far.

But all that ends for Jack with this particular session. It became "an orgy of shouting, cursing, and intolerant discourtesy. The only way to interject an opinion was to out-shout the rest. Even then, no one could have heard or would have heard what was said." Jack was hurt during this argument particularly by another student Rex's characterization of him as "the last of the old Civil War veterans." He also was surprised and angered by the level of profanity. "I have been amazed and even embarrassed to hear some of the words used in class by both males and females, Whites, Blacks, and even by Dr. Kranz."

Jack talked with Pete Kranz about what had happened. He described his hurt feelings and his being offended by Ann and Carlton's behavior, and that of others in the class. "Dr. Kranz was not distressed," Jack writes. "He expressed the opinion that situations of that type often can have good effects. Sometimes when people are angry, they will show emotions that they themselves might be unaware of or, if aware, have been suppressing." Pete went on to explain that some of the deepest misconceptions, fears, and dislikes of members of other racial groups could be combatted only if they were addressed directly...not with silence, not with wordless resentment and quiet fuming; rather with unshielded answers that were statements of direct emotional truth.

Things had calmed down by the time the next class session began. After half an hour, Jack felt that the students had returned to "their usual selves." They discussed the incident from the previous class and, as Jack puts it, "all listened politely." That is, until the brawl broke out once again. Ann led the way. In a later interview, she explained her motivation in conversations like this one. "Sometimes it was just anger, because I felt that a lot of my time was being wasted with people just superficially talking...you know, skim over everything, but don't really get to the bone, to the meat of it. You're sitting there trying to really say, 'This is what I am feeling,' and not only does the other person not relate to what you are feeling, he doesn't let you know what *he* is feeling."

More of the black students joined in on the shouting, with abrasive language, much of it aimed directly at Jack as it broadened to a blistering assessment of the racial attitudes of all the white people in the room. The Whites responded in kind, disparaging Blacks with frequent use of the word "niggers," often preceded by equally caustic adjectives.

With this, Pete felt he should intervene. Things were getting too rough, and he worried that actual violence could result. He stopped the discussion. He then broke the class up into smaller separate groups of two to four students, and asked that they go over the two brawls with each other and determine what each of them had gotten from them.

Pete placed Jack and Ann together in their own separate conversation. Jack quickly sat down next to Ann, wanting to speak with her. "The only way for me not to carry a grudge is to confront the person whom I feel has caused my anger." Jack wanted to have his "say," as he called it. He had been shouted down. He felt he had not been listened to by the Blacks who had been doing so much of the shouting. He expected Ann would still be angry and still intent on making her views heard by the one man whose opinions of Blacks had opened her heart and its anger. He felt compelled to try to get her to see "'where I was coming from,'" as he confides to his journal, "the term so often used in class."

To his surprise, Ann responded to him with considerable grace. "She heard me out," he writes, "and even referred to herself in the situation as a devil's advocate." Jack admitted that he had thought the same thing during the brawls. "We spoke frankly during that private conversation of many things, and the fact is I left her side reluctantly." Jack wanted more conversation. The class was ending, and as he walked out the door, he realized that, indeed, he was grateful to Ann. Her bravery, her direct intensity, and even her often profane speech had taken on the quality of direct truth-telling for Jack that became more evident as she treated him in their private conversation with such kind, although still very direct, open-heartedness.

"I hope she regards me equally as well," he writes.

—

Terry was a white student in the class in 1975. In class discussions, he prided himself on being direct and unwavering. "Today, there was a lot of hostility," he writes. "People start getting fed up when the person talking is obviously playing games. Being evasive. Not telling the truth. All that. I hope I don't come across as playing games, because I wouldn't be there if I weren't sincere. I drive a hundred miles a day in order to be in that class, and I wouldn't do it if I didn't care. So if I start playing games, I want people to tell me."

As with almost everyone in class, the racial anger that was inevitably exposed during discussions was for Terry difficult to accept in himself. He reflects upon his own racism. "The poison is so deep, you keep covering it up, and you don't realize what you're doing. It's easy, then, to let your old feelings come back. Especially when, on a day like today, people are taking so many pot shots."

Terry mentions his reading in Eldridge Cleaver's *Soul On Ice*, one of the required texts for the class. Written while Cleaver was an inmate in the Folsom State Prison in California, it was published in 1968. It remains to this day a seminal document from the American Civil Rights movement, and deals in part with what white people do not understand about black people. "Cleaver said, 'You don't have to teach people how to be human. You have to teach them how to stop being inhuman,'" Terry writes in his journal. He mentions an aspect of Cleaver's remark that he has noticed with every session of the class, and that he would like to incorporate into his own life. "Black people are faced all their lives with this struggle every day…and I have a hard time handling it after six weeks. What would life be for me if I were black? How would I act, and what would my feelings be? I don't care how far I come. I will never be able to identify completely with the black race because of my own identity as a White. But I can learn to be aware."

Terry recalls in his journal an event from that year's Halloween, when, in the middle of his home visit, he was entrusted with the care of his home host's five year-old, for their trick-or-treat circuit of the neighborhood. "It was an experience for me doing that in the black community. One lady wouldn't trust her son to go around with me and my host's little boy because I was white, and she didn't know me. This was funny, because her 'trust' sounded a lot like the white 'trust' that I was so familiar with, when it comes to black people."

———

Patricia began berating a fellow student, Vickie, who was actually half Puerto Rican. Patricia was angry at Vickie for siding too much with the Whites in the class. "Puerto Rican! You think that, as far as they're concerned, you're any different from us?"

Vickie began weeping. The rest of the class knew that she was indeed a Latina and that she was married to a white Navy man. "I've lived all my life with my own people," she said, "or in Navy communities. I've never had to really face the issues of racialism."

Patricia and some of the other Blacks in the class laughed outright at this, even deriding the claim.

"And that's why I think your problems aren't such big problems," Vickie said.

"What?"

"They don't seem that immense to me."

A donnybrook of argument ensued. All the Blacks in the class rallied to Patricia's side, to explain to Vickie how deep the problems Patricia was describing actually were. Vickie's tears continued although, despite her unhappiness, she remained insistent on her assertion that Patricia's life could not be all that bad.

Even a few of the Whites in the class felt that Vickie couldn't be telling the truth. One of them interrupted the argument. "You're a member of a minority. Maybe you've been exposed to enough prejudices that you've built—"

"I have not!"

"Or are trying to build, a shield of 'I don't care' around yourself—"

"What do you know about it?"

"—without realizing it, see?"

"What could you *possibly* know about any of that?"

—

A black male student, addressing a white male student: "What you don't realize or understand is the reluctance of Blacks to reveal themselves, least of all to Whites. And of course the way Whites handle it is to just ignore the Blacks and their problems."

—

"I'm mad at all this." The student, a white male, folds his arms before him as a kind of barrier. "I don't like dealing with what we're dealing with. It's embarrassing."
 "Your racism is…that's all it is? Just embarrassing?"
 "Having to deal with it, yes. I'd rather not deal with these fears."
 "Fears!"
 "Yeah, I'd prefer—"
 "You're in denial, man!"
 "What?"
 "You don't know who you are."

—

A black woman, addressing all the Whites in the classroom: "I don't trust you white liberals, and I fear that a number of people in this class are just that. I'm not talking about a truly liberal person. I'm talking about the so-called 'white liberal,' who really is just showing off. They don't want to be confronted with the truth…the truth being that they are just as prejudiced as everyone else."

—

A black woman interrupts a white student who has been complaining about the tendency of Blacks to feel sorry for themselves. "It never ceases to amaze me how the white man never really wants to see the actual situation Blacks are condemned to."

"What we hear is a lot of complaining."

"Complaining! How do you condone this?"

"Yeah, it's up to you to help yourself. We're not responsible for—"

"How can you feel that a living, breathing human with darker skin can be subhuman?"

"I don't think you're subhuman."

"How do you justify to yourself this kind of cruelty?"

—

One of the books assigned to the class was James Forman's *Sammy Younge Jr.: The First Black College Student to Die in the Black Liberation Movement.* On the night of January 3, 1966, Younge stopped at a white-run Standard Oil gas station in Macon County, Alabama. He needed to go to the bathroom. The white station attendant, Marvin Segrest, forebade Younge to use the whites-only facility, and an argument between the two men ensued. Eventually Segrest pulled a gun on Younge and shot him dead. Younge was twenty-one years old, a student at Tuskegee Institute, and a veteran of the U.S. Navy. He was actively involved in the Student Non-Violent Coordinating Committee and the Mississippi Freedom Democratic Party's efforts to register black voters. Segrest's trial for murder lasted one hour and ten minutes. An all-white male jury acquitted him of the crime.

While in class, discussing Younge's fate, one of the white students quotes the author James Forman: "'No white man has ever, in the legal history of this country, been tried, convicted and executed for the murder of any black man, woman, or child.'" The student nods. "I don't doubt the truth of this statement. I know that I cannot recall ever hearing or reading of such a case. The surprising part is that I've never even given it any thought."

"So what do you think you've got here, then," a male black student suddenly says. "Just another dead Nigger?"

"No, of course not. I—"

"Listen, maybe *you* haven't thought about any of this. But imagine if you're a black person in an argument with some white guy, and it's getting hotter and hotter, and you know way down inside that it's almost impossible to convict a white man for any offense against a Black."

"But—"

"That's futility, man! And then this white boy pulls out a club and attacks me, and kills me. Nothing will happen to him. He gets to go free. No conviction. No jail time. But I'm going to defend myself, and if I get the club away from him and hit him…and he dies…I'm in jail forever."

—

"What'd you say?"

"Well…of the Blacks I've gotten to know both in the class and from my home visit, I have found no 'bad or super Niggers.'"

"What?"

"Yeah, your people appear to have the same limitations as us."

"You mean, as you Whites."

"Yeah. I can't believe it."

"That we're just as limited."

"Yeah!"

—

A young white woman from Jacksonville, a devout Protestant Christian, complains one day about the language in class, language used even in some of the assigned books.

"I thought this was a university," she says. "But of the five books we've read, three have been filled with profanity."

"What's wrong with that?" a black woman says.

"Not just 'Hell' or 'Damn,' but rather some of the filthiest words that I know of."

"So? What do you think we're talking about here?"

"I thought this was a university class."

"It is! But it's a class about one group of people enslaving another, and then grinding them down and down. That's what's profane! Shit, Girl, that's the language of it!"

The white woman sits back, silent a moment. "Terms I've never heard before."

"Girl!"

"Or at least only when men—"

"Girl, you—"

"Never in mixed company."

"You need to listen to black women talk."

—

A black male student with a large Afro is asked by a white male student about the Black Liberation Army (also known as the BLA.) A black nationalist organization in the 1970s, it was made up of many former members of the Black Panthers. Its purpose was to enter into armed struggle with the U.S. government.

"I mean, you talk about racism against Blacks," the white student says. "That's a racist organization, too, isn't it?"

"Look, since so many Whites think that racial tension in Jacksonville is motivated by the Black Liberation Army, I know that I must be on my guard. With my appearance, I could easily be taken in by the cops, even though I have no connection with the BLA. But that's the kind of shit that white redneck racist motherfuckers pull, see? And every time I think about this, I think about what would be done if this were the WLA, the White Liberation Army, going around killing black people. I know they wouldn't be harassed at all, and that's the type of thing that makes me hate Whites."

—

A young white supremacist is asked why he feels such intense hatred for black people. The questioner is a young, very dark black man, wearing impenetrable sunglasses. He has professed that he believes in the "Hate Whitey!" idea.

"You ask me why?" the white student replies. "Here's why. The Blacks want a free ride just because they have black skin."

"A free ride?"

"Right. Sure they've had a lot of bad done to them. But I'm not responsible for that, and that's why they piss me off."

"You're not responsible."

"No, I can't get used to that idea at all. And with guys like you, I'm... all of us Whites, we're *all* on trial, all the time."

"That's the truth, man, and you deserve to be."

"Why? Here I am, telling you the truth. Now! And you're sitting there behind those shades, and I can't tell what you're thinking. You're hiding from me."

"We live in conflict. All the time. Our feelings, they're right below the surface, and they're liable to explode at any time. Composure? Fuck composure!"

"I want to see your eyes."

"The shades are necessary, man. The cool. You'd understand that if you realized the cost of the suffering we go through to maintain that cool."

"That's a lot of intellectual shit."

"And just now I've realized how all the animosity, defense, and prejudice on your part is evidence of a sick, cruel, decrepit, closed mind that tends to destroy rather than bind people together."

—

Occasionally, Pete Kranz gets involved, especially as he is reading the students' journals. He has read this white supremacist's journal entries, and in the open space at the bottom of a page, he writes the following: "You've got a lot to say. So, say it! You need greater depth and self-exploration. Who are you trying to convince...you? Go do it! Get beneath the surface. Expose yourself to yourself. Let yourself go."

—

Two black men are talking for the class about their views of being black.

"Black is the diagnosis; uncertain is the prognosis."

"Yeah, but that means that you've got to be worried all the time just about being black."

"What else is there?"

"Education. Pride. Hard work."

"Listen, you're still black, one hundred percent of the time."

"But look, there's—"

"You not only have to be aware of the Whites. Sometimes it's the Blacks who are trying to get ahead at all cost."

"Yeah, maybe so. But they're fighting for crumbs, man."

"I know that. But if it means stepping on other Blacks, then that's what he'll do."

—

A white male student defends the Jacksonville police department's treatment of black people. "They're doing a good job. It's tough out there."

"Listen," a black student says. "They've always had an assassination squad, and its function has been to eliminate the 'uppity Niggers' that they can't railroad into prisons."

—

A white female student asks a black female student, "Would you date a white man?"

"I'm often fighting with...with my inner feelings."

"What do you mean?"

"I keep telling myself that I'm not prejudiced. But I can't conceive of a white man touching me. I mean, I did date a white man once or twice. But every time he tried to touch me, I became cold as ice. I could never let him touch me. It's not that I think I'm 'too good;' rather it's something I just can't explain."

—

A white male student describes his father's joking to friends that the young man "is going to be living with those Niggers for a week."

A black female student replies, "It's sad to think that this class, this city, this state, and even the nation are going nowhere as a direct result of people like your father."

—

Karl, a white student, and also an army recruiter, spoke English with an accent. He was asked by one of the black students what his preconceptions of black people were.

"I didn't come to this class with any preconceptions."

"Sure you did, man. You're white!"

"I see what's going on here in the South, and I just can't stand it."

"But you're *still* white, and you can do something about it."

"I—"

"You've got the power."

"A number of my family members were in concentration camps."

"What?"

"I'm a Jew."

"Oh...I...I'm sorry, I didn't—"

"The Holocaust."

"Yeah. I know. See, I didn't...I didn't—"

"When I came to this country, I couldn't understand why someone would hate someone else because of the color of his skin."

—

A conversation between an older white male student and several younger black students, men and women:

"When you were a kid," one of the black students says, "how did you address older Blacks."

"'Uncle.' 'Aunt.'"

"Did you ever use 'Mr.' or 'Mrs.'?

"No. It was okay for me to call a Black who was thirty years or so my senior by his first name."

"What about with a white person."

"No, no. With them it was always Mr. This or Mrs. That."

"And those old radio programs. I mean, did you like Amos and Andy when you were young?"

"I did, yes."

"Stepin Fetchit?"

"Him, too."

"What do white people say? 'I declare, black boy, you as slow as molasses in January.'"

"Well, I don't know about that."

"Jam-up and Honey?"

"They were great. The Grand Ol' Opry on the radio? Sure! They were funny."

"Those two guys were white! You know that, don't you? In black face."

"Yeah. I know."

"Do you know how obvious it is that those characters determined your feelings about race?"

"They were playing at it, sure, but that was irrelevant."

"Irrelevant!"

"They were funny!"

"You don't think they were characters invented by racists?"

"Well, if the show had been interpreted to mean that those characters were representative of the black race only, then certainly it would have been wrong."

"And you don't think that was the case."

"I have real trouble believing that."

—

A white female student recounted in class how she had always believed that black men were rapists.

"All of them?" a black male responded.

"All kinds of things. Bad treatment of women. Attack. Disrespect."

"Where'd you get that?"

"That all they've ever wanted was a white woman."

"Look here, I've never had a white woman in my life!"

"So you're the exception."

"No! I never wanted one. You're up there on that pedestal of yours—"

"Pedestal!"

"Yes. All you white women."

—

A young black male student: "I haven't talked too much or monopolized the class time or anything. But on several occasions, even after waiting until no one else is talking, or when a question has been asked, and no one else has an answer to it except for me, I get shushed and waved aside."

—

A white male student: "I've dealt with Blacks one way or another all my life. I mean, I played with a couple of them as a little kid, at my house and at theirs. There was no racial consciousness."

"On your part, or theirs?"

"Mine! What do you think? That was the only consciousness I had."

"Did you ever talk about race?"

"Sometimes. Like when we went to see Tarzan movies."

"What did you talk about?"

"I wanted to know what those black kids felt when Tarzan would take on a whole group of natives."

"What'd they say?"

"I wanted to know, since the natives were black, did my friends feel any different about them than I did."

"And?"

"One boy's answer had something to do with Tarzan being the hero of the story."

"So?"

"He said Tarzan was the hero, and so he himself had no sympathy for the natives."

"Bullshit!"

"That's what he said! You want me to lie to you?"

—

In the midst of a particularly fractious argument in class, a black female student, who has been listening quietly, suddenly interrupts. "Sometimes I feel so super-turned-off and militant that I can't stand myself. Why do I feel so much more frustration sitting here now than I did a year ago? I believe that the older I get, the more angry I get." She leans forward and gestures to a couple of the white students seated in the circle. "It never ceases to amaze me how the white man never really wants to see the actual situation in which Blacks are condemned to live." The woman surveys the entire circle. "Blindness! And some of you white people here today appear to not even want to look at yourselves, because you fear what you might see."

Moments later, she is still nonplussed, and interrupts again. "Do I become angry simply because of what you—" She points at one of the white male students. "What you have actually done to me—"

"I haven't done anything to you."

"What *you* are actually doing to me right now? Or because you are white? Simply the condition of your being white. Has the system corrupted my judgment so much?"

—

During a class session, a black female student offers to a white female classmate her opinion of white women.

"We don't like your long hair, and we don't like your sexual habits."

"What habits?"

"Oral sex. We don't do that."

"That's racism on your part."

"What do you mean?"

"I don't give oral sex, and you just assumed that I do. You didn't even ask me. That's racism."

—

"If I woke up tomorrow and there were no black people in the world, would I care?"

"Fuck you, white boy. And fuck your waking up."

—

A white male student, in his early thirties, born and raised in the South, holds up his copy of *The Autobiography of Malcolm X* and displays it to the other students. "Where do you think he gets this shit?"

A black woman student gathers her hands before her on a table. Her voice shakes. "Not the same place where you get yours, that's for sure."

THE HOME VISIT

"The only other time I had an opportunity to visit a white person's home was to clean up or do housework. This was very different."
—a black student.

"They put me in the same room with two of their young children. That was a sermon of trust."
—a white student.

History plays a significant role in the soul of each of us, whether we know in fine detail what happened in the past or indeed know few of the details. An anecdotal collective consciousness informs our lives from the very moment of our first breath. In the southern regions of the United States, this is so clear a condition that everyone there must take it into account, even in everyday decisions. It is true to this day, and was demonstrably so in

Jacksonville during the years leading up to 1972 and the launch of Pete Kranz's classes. Presuppositions and prejudices about race were very much a part of the mindset of those students who were thinking about taking the class.

But there was also one other element that had motivated many of the students to take the class, Blacks and Whites alike. It was perceived that this class would be an easy "A." Not a lot of reading. Very little writing required, other than the journal. No tests. No quizzes. No final exam. But the students were unaware of a few requirements in the class that, although having little to do with the normal kinds of educational rigor, would come as a singular shock to almost all of them.

Those things came into sharp focus on the first day of the class, when Pete told the students what he in fact *would* require them to do.

—

In 1972, Judi, whom we met earlier in this book, had separated from her husband, and had a two year-old boy. She had a few years of college study, and entered the new university with the idea of completing her Bachelor's degree. Like other suddenly single women with kids, a balanced budget was a difficult thing to achieve, and Judi had no intention of shirking her responsibilities to her little boy. She returned with him to her parents' home in Jacksonville, and the two lived in a small apartment over the garage.

Judi well knew the racial territory inhabited by the citizens, white and black, of Jacksonville in 1972: "Nearly all of us in the class had grown up in a segregated society. The laws had changed, but attitudes hadn't. Integration meant busing. I had been raised with a very white upbringing, and had never gone to school with Blacks. We attended different churches, lived in different neighborhoods, ate at different lunch counters, used different toilets and water fountains, swam in different pools, went to different beaches, and lived in different circumstances. UNF was to be my first experience in an integrated setting. We didn't mix, marry, or have friendships with people of a different color. And that kind of mixing wasn't just frowned upon; it had once been against the law. Most of us hadn't even worked with black people. We were separate, and not equal. 'Out of sight, out of mind' was no doubt the intention of segregation."

Jim Crow was a matter of fact, and one particular organization had taken it upon itself to make sure that those laws remained enforced. The Ku Klux Klan, founded in 1866 and in existence to this day, is a loose-knit organization of white nationalists devoted to the supremacy of white people in the United States. Reading its history, one is impressed by the unyielding intensity of the Klan's hate-filled philosophy and by the organization's readiness to commit acts of severe violence against anyone, white or black, who opposes it. Murder is its ultimate weapon, and many hundreds of people, mostly black, have been killed by members of the Klan, even into contemporary times. In just the ten years before the founding of the University of North Florida, the organization was responsible for a few of the most famous crimes ever to be committed against particular Blacks... and some Whites.

Medgar Evers was a well-known organizer for the National Association for the Advancement of Colored People in Mississippi. Returning on the morning of June 12, 1963 from an NAACP meeting, he was assassinated by rifle fire in the driveway of his home. The murderer, a white man named Byron De La Beckwith, avoided immediate conviction for the crime. The deliberating juries in the initial two trials were comprised of white men only. (Black people, not allowed to vote, were thus not allowed to join juries, since you had to be on the voting rolls to qualify.) De La Beckwith was finally convicted of killing Evers in 1994.

On September 15, 1963, four black girls were killed in the bombing of the Sixteenth Street Baptist Church in Birmingham, Alabama. Twenty-two other individuals were injured in that attack. Reverend Martin Luther King Jr. described it as "one of the most vicious and tragic crimes ever perpetrated against humanity." Three of the four accused white perpetrators were convicted of murder, one in 1977, two others in 2001 and 2002.

Pete Kranz's boyhood friend Michael Schwerner was murdered by Klansmen, along with his two Congress of Racial Equality colleagues James Chaney and Andrew Goodman, in Mississippi in the summer of 1964.

During the same period in 1964, two black teenagers, Henry Hezekia Dee and Charles Eddie Moore, were picked up hitchhiking by members of the Klan outside Meadville, Mississippi. They were tortured by their abductors, weighted down by machinery tied to their bodies and, still alive, thrown into the Mississippi River. Ironically, their bodies were discovered by FBI agents during their search for Schwerner, Chaney, and Goodwin. James Ford Seale, a member of the Ku Klux Klan, was convicted of the murders of the two teenagers in 2007.

In 1965, a white Detroit mother of five children, Viola Liuzzo, was in Alabama to attend a civil rights demonstration. Returning from a trip to the Montgomery airport, to which she had given other activists a ride, she was pursued by, and shot dead from, a car that contained four members of the Ku Klux Klan. Three of them were convicted of murder in 1967. The fourth was an FBI informant whose testimony helped in the conviction of the others. He was set free and, under an assumed identity, lived until 1998.

In 1966, Vernon Dahmer, a black man who had been a close friend as a youth of Medgar Evers, died from injuries he sustained during a gasoline firebomb attack of his home by several members of the Klan. Dahmer had been president of the local NAACP chapter in Forrest County, Mississippi, and very active in the effort to register Blacks to vote. The same Klansman, Sam Bowers, who had ordered the apprehending of Michael Schwerner and his associates two years earlier was implicated in the murder of Vernon Dahmer. Four trials of Bowers ended in mistrials, and he remained free until finally being convicted as one of Dahmer's murderers in 1998.

In 1967, the Jackson, Mississippi residences of a white Methodist layman civil rights activist named Robert Kochtitzky and a Jewish rabbi named Perry Nusbaum were bombed by members of the Klan. This extension of Klan violence to white Jews was part of a broadening of the general Klan effort to keep the United States pure white, "Christian" (an association underscored by the Klan's use of the burning cross,) and anti-immigrant.

In 1968, Martin Luther King Jr. was assassinated, and violence immediately broke out in one hundred twenty-six U.S. cities.

(One certain indicator of the lasting influence of Jim Crow attitudes in the South is the amount of time it took to seek and secure convictions for many of the crimes mentioned above. A further note: A Southern Poverty Law Center report released in 2015 listed one hundred forty organized KKK groups currently active in the southern United States, five of which are based in Florida.)

It is important to note that no one in Judi's family had any involvement with the Ku Klux Klan. But because of that organization's long public history of anti-Black rhetoric and proven violence against black people, coupled with the collusion of many state and local governments and their efforts to impose Jim Crow restrictions, the organization was viewed, particularly by black people, as a kind of ad hoc, last ditch enforcer of those restrictions in the South. In 1972, the notion of white nativism remained an extremely strong one within a large percentage of the white population in the region.

Ann, who was black, had grown up with a set of expectations for white people similar to those for Blacks that Judi had heard as a child. Ann wrote about this in her class journal: "Assumptions work both ways. For Blacks, the following statements seem to ring true: all Whites are racists. All Whites are rich. They smell sickly-sweet or like a wet dog. They sleep in twin beds. Their dogs are weapons against the Nigger. White women all want black men, and all white men want to rape black women."

Also in her journal she describes the emotional effects on her family of two hundred fifty years of actual slavery, and another hundred of Jim Crow. She knew that black women had been lynched by white crowds, as had black men. Jim Crow had conditioned Blacks to never look a white person directly in the eye. A black man could be killed just for looking suggestively at a white woman, as had been the famous fate of fourteen year-old Emmett Till, who had committed such a heinous offense in August, 1955 in Money, Mississippi.

From Chicago, Emmett was visiting relatives in Money, and one day spoke on the street with Carolyn Bryant, a young white woman who was married to a local storeowner Roy Bryant. Carolyn told her husband about Emmett's flirtatious suggestions, and a few nights later, Roy and his half-brother, J.W. Milan, entered the home of Emmett's great-uncle, where the boy was staying. The white men were armed, and they abducted Emmett.

Later that night, the two men attacked, physically mutilated, and then shot the boy to death. They dumped his body into the Tallahatchie River.

Emmett's body was recovered three days later, and returned to Chicago. His mother described what she saw when the coffin containing the boy's body was opened: "There was just no way I could describe what was in that box. No way." She insisted that, at Emmett's funeral, the casket remain open for public viewing. "I just wanted the world to see."

Emmett Till had been so savagely beaten that he was unrecognizable. Photos of his body in the coffin were distributed to news organizations across the country, and the trial that followed the arrests of his murderers was covered by all major U.S. newspapers and magazines.

At the end of the trial, which was held in Sumner, Mississippi, the defendants, Roy Bryant and J. W. Milan, were acquitted of the crime of murder by a jury of twelve white men. A few months later, a grand jury decided not to indict the two men for the lesser crime of kidnapping, despite their own testimony that they had abducted Till from his great-uncle's home.

Ann remembered the interview she read years later, that had been given by the two murderers to *Look* magazine in 1956. In the interview J. W. Milan said, "I'm no bully; I never hurt a Nigger in my life. I like Niggers—in their place—I know how to work 'em. But I just decided it was time a few people got put on notice. As long as I live and can do anything about it, Niggers are gonna stay in their place."

About his confronting Emmett the night he shot the boy, Milan admitted to saying, "Chicago boy...I'm tired of 'em sending your kind down here to stir up trouble. Goddam you, I'm going to make an example of you—just so everybody can know how me and my folks stand."

Milan admitted in the interview that he had indeed murdered Emmett Till. Bryant insisted for the rest of his life upon his own innocence in the crime. Because of laws against double jeopardy, Bryant and Milan remained free, and they both died peacefully many years later.

—

In 1972, memories of all the events mentioned here were fresh on the minds, in one way or another, of the students entering Pete Kranz's class. The idea of the class fascinated Judi and Ann, because it held the possibility for experiences that had heretofore been beyond anything that either woman knew. The home visit was to be one of these experiences. When she first saw a description of it, Judi barely believed what she was reading. "It was amazing that the university ever allowed Dr. Kranz to teach this class. The home visit? It had never been done before."

The term itself is rather bland. It has the innocent sound of other such terms ("field trip," "museum visit," "a tour of the library," etc.) A brief moment outside the classroom that presents few, if any, challenges, and that usually will be in some way fun.

As Pete was explaining the ground rules of the class to his first 1972 students, he brought up the home visit. Each student would be required to live in the home of a member, or members, of the other race for a full week. Pete waited as, at first in silence, the students absorbed what, in so few words, he had just said. Then there were exhalations, nervous mutters and laughter, more silence, and exchanged glances one student to the next.

So Judi would stay in the Jacksonville home of a black family. She knew little about how black people lived. Her parents had never allowed her to enter a black person's home. It simply was not permitted. "Most Whites were quite familiar with statements such as 'They are lazy,'" she says. "'They're less intelligent. They can't be trusted. They're dirty and they smell.'"

The average white person in Jacksonville at the time would most probably agree with Judi's father: "He would tell me, 'As far as their intelligence, that's just the way they are. They can't help it. Their brains are smaller. Even if you give them a decent place to live, they'll soon trash it and turn it into a ghetto.' I had never challenged these ideas."

Given this history, Judi felt right away that a certain leap in willingness was going to be required for her to take the class. The "A" grade she expected was not going to come so easily.

Patricia, whom we have met because of her friendship with Martha ("that woman from Macclennny"), had clear expectations about white people. "One Sunday, I talked to one of my brothers about the home visit. I was apprehensive about it. He said that it's easy to stay with someone and pretend you like them. I told him it's not as easy as he thinks. In this class, I've discovered how difficult it is to do, especially when you're going through a mind change, as I've been doing. The conscious mind starts having conflicts with the subconscious, and it becomes struggle on top of struggle." She made the decision to continue attending the class nonetheless, home visit or not, even though the idea of staying in a white family's home for a full week, unprotected, gave her considerable pause.

"The home visit was essential," Pete explains. He knew that none of the students had ever participated in such an endeavor, as had few of the home visit hosts. In the case of the hosts, Pete had a particularly difficult task. Simply finding homes that would be willing to put up a person about whom the hosts had no previous knowledge, for a full week, was a big order. That that person was a member of the other race made the search even more problematic, given the overall state of race relations in Jacksonville at the time. As so many of the white students said, simply mixing with Blacks was largely forbidden, out of custom or habit, if not still illegal. There is a long and honored tradition among southern black families of providing shelter and sustenance to black travelers in the South who were not allowed to stay in white-owned hotels or boarding houses. Such accommodations were the norm for Blacks traveling in the South well into the second half of the twentieth century. But in those cases, the travelers themselves were all black. Few Whites ever stayed in those black-owned private accommodations. So, here too, despite the tradition of black hospitality in private homes, that hospitality was seldom to be enjoyed by white people.

One of the students later interviewed says, "Yes, Pete Kranz is a very persuasive individual, a man on a mission who will not take 'no' for an answer. But what he was asking of people was huge." Besides the racial issues that this course requirement brought up, there were significant others as well. "Some of the possible home hosts that he spoke with would have refused for valid reasons. But there were also more personal, more prejudicial reasons for saying 'no.' How would the rest of the family react? How welcome would black students be in a white neighborhood...and vice versa?" Pete was to display a personality trait that most of his students came to recognize and value. This same student says of Pete's effort to find lodging for the home visits, "If he got 'no' for an answer, he'd ask that person for a recommendation of someone else to ask, and he'd just keep on rolling."

As it happened, most of the host families were from the middle class, Whites and Blacks alike. This same former student points out in her interview that several white students felt that their home stay would have been more challenging if they had been lodged in Jacksonville's very poor ghettoized black communities. Some black students felt that they would have learned more were they to spend the week with outright white racists. "That wasn't feasible," Pete says. "A hostile environment, probably on both sides. Safety considerations. It was to be difficult enough in ways that could not be predicted. There had to be a starting point, and we consciously pursued families from the middle class."

Forty-five families participated in the home visits over the life of the program. In an interview, one of the white hosts explains some of the concerns of her family during the home visit. The worries are actually rather pedestrian, but what makes them nonetheless interesting is that hosts from both races mentioned similar concerns. "What students and hosts have in common," Pete says, "we discovered are the same sort of apprehensions, but seen from the other side of the mirror." Hosts worry over the comfort of their guests. Is the neighborhood safe for her? Food…what do we feed him? Sometimes the student wonders what he/she will be expected to eat. Hosts asked themselves, do we prepare just our regular kinds of meals? Do we eat black, or do we eat white? "The preparation and sharing of food is an intimate gesture," one host recalls. "And some students anticipated this and shied away from it initially, arranging to arrive just after the end of the meal." Students asked themselves, do I help with the dishes? Can I do my laundry there?

With all those questions, most of the participants, black and white, recall that that shared intimacy, pedestrian or not, and especially in the privacy of a family environment, became one of the important experiences to be gained from the entire class. One host who a few years earlier had actually also been a student in the class, pointed out that "sitting down at a table, next to or across from strangers, can be daunting. While one can occupy the mouth while eating, the eyes are bound to meet at one point or another, which will lead the conversation beyond 'Could you pass the salt, please?'"

—

No home visit, by Blacks or Whites, was the same as any other. There are occasional similar elements mentioned in the journals and subsequent interviews, from one student or home host to the next. But almost all the visits are notable for their individuality and the powerful emotional effect the visit had, on students and hosts alike, no matter their race.

A black student, Dwight, had a complicated visit that he felt at first would be a playact on the parts of all the participants, himself included.

"I was completely shocked to know that one of the requirements of the class was to stay in a white home. But after thinking it over, I figured it should prove interesting. Not knowing what to expect, I pictured that I would get the red carpet treatment. The white people would pull out all the old sheets and pillow cases because The Nigger was coming. But someone would brief the family on certain rules to be followed that week, and the family would put on a super-liberal act...that I would read right through. The Whites would put me in a cornered-off part of the house so they could keep tabs on The Nigger's activity."

Dwight bolstered his confidence with what he felt he already knew about white people: "I thought I would not be able to trust any of them. I had to keep my guard up, no matter how the Whites seemed. After all, I had been conditioned to distrust Whites, and I wasn't about to be taken in!"

Dwight's first contact with the family (whom I will call Mr. and Mrs. Beltran, their college-age daughter Pauline, and their college-age son) took place in a UNF parking lot. His expectation was shaken right away, since his initiation to the Beltran family was through Pauline: "I hadn't met her parents yet. I must admit, when I first made her acquaintance, I just knew she had money and a 'bad ride'...a nice car, in other words. Later that day,

I found out that none of this expectation was true. There was no bad ride either. I had to carry her home in my car."

The sight of a white woman riding in the front seat of a car driven by a black man was rare in Jacksonville. Dwight noticed that his car was getting unusual scrutiny from many of the students as he maneuvered through the parking lot: "People stared at us. It made me feel uneasy, and I wondered how Pauline was feeling. I glanced over to see. To tell the truth, I don't think she noticed the stares we were getting."

The two students talked with each other during the ride to Pauline's home. The conversation was friendly, an exchange of descriptions of the different classes they were taking, what subjects they liked, what they didn't care for…the usual for students just entering new classes, with little truly personal exchange. But the atmosphere changed as Dwight and Pauline approached the house in which she lived with her parents. "I saw a lady in the yard. She was smiling and gave me a hearty welcome into the house. She was Pauline's mother, Mrs. Beltran. She appeared very friendly and honest, traits that I later found to be quite truthful."

Mrs. Beltran escorted Dwight into the house and took him immediately to the bedroom that would be his for the week. "As I went to put my things away, I was surprised to find that I was sleeping in their son's bed, and that he was to sleep in the den."

Pauline's brother was not much in evidence during the first two days of Dwight's visit. When he did arrive on the scene, Dwight was to encounter the first hint of mistrust, even of dislike, from anyone in the family. Despite his initial absence, the young man's presence in the family was made obvious when his pet was introduced to Dwight on that first day of the home visit. "At dinner, I was introduced to other members of the family, except for the son, who was not home at the time. I *was* introduced to a large Doberman Pinscher, the son's dog, who I thought at first would try to include me in his menu."

Dwight's reaction was not unusual for a black person living in the South. The large, aggressively trained dog has been a figure of fierce authority since slavery began in the American colonies. Used by slave owners and, after slavery, by white vigilante groups, police, and others to intimidate scofflaws, prisoners and, most pointedly, black people in general, such dogs inspired real fear. A singular illustration of why that was so can be found in the famous newsreel films and newspaper photos of the Children's Crusade of early May 1963, in Birmingham, Alabama.

Dr. Martin Luther King Jr. and the Southern Christian Leadership Conference had determined that Birmingham was a prime target for their efforts to desegregate southern cities, since it was, as King said, "probably the most thoroughly segregated city in the United States." In 1960, Blacks accounted for forty percent of the city's population, although only ten percent of the black population was registered to vote. The per-capita unemployment rate for Blacks was two and one-half times higher than that for Whites. King and the SCLC's efforts would be intended to desegregate Birmingham's downtown stores, bring about fair hiring practices, make public parks accessible to all, desegregate public schools, libraries, lunch counters, and white churches, and bring about a thoroughly effective black voter registration drive.

Adhering to Dr. King's philosophy of non-violence, so many demonstrators were arrested during these SCLC Birmingham demonstrations that the local jails began to fill. National news outlets publicized all this, successfully showing the peaceful determination of the black demonstrators to have their views acknowledged. Dr. King himself and many others were arrested on April 12, 1963, and his time in a cell was memorialized by his famous "Letter from Birmingham Jail," in which he wrote, "We know through painful experience that freedom is never voluntarily given by the oppressor; it must be demanded by the oppressed."

Between May 2 and May 5, the Birmingham city jails became packed with demonstrator/prisoners. Thousand of black pupils and young students had left school, and gathered at the Sixteenth Street Baptist Church for instructions about the non-violent march they were to make, with the purpose of being peacefully arrested for civil disobedience. Once under way, they were regularly attacked by city firemen using fire hoses in an attempt to disperse the crowd. At the same time, the Birmingham Commissioner of Public Safety, Theophilus Eugene "Bull" Connor, also allowed the police use of German Shepherds to attack the children who were demonstrating.

Connor's philosophy can be summed up by his remark, "I ain't gonna segregate no Niggers and Whites together in this town." The photos and films of those attacks clearly demonstrate why a large dog whose breed has a reputation for fierce behavior and has been trained for attack, could be a threat to any black person. (A side note: Bull Connor himself had run for mayor of Birmingham, also in 1963, on April 2. He was quoted as saying that, if elected, he would purchase one hundred new police dogs "for use in the event of more Freedom Rides." Connor's statements did little to help his campaign, and he lost the election.)

So when Dwight encountered the Doberman Pinscher in the Beltran family's dining room, he felt the home visit had reached a new, clear phase. *"There it is, the white weapon,* I thought to myself." Even so, as the dinner progressed, so did the conversation, and Dwight was left alone by the Doberman. Dwight found himself included in the talk. To his surprise, "after dinner, we sat around the table and rapped about race, school, and other problems in the world. I found that I could even joke with these white folks."

The conviviality was muffled, though, at dinner the following night.

"I was introduced to another white man, Steve, who was one of Pauline's boyfriends. He offered his hand, and I extended mine. As we began to shake, he remarked, 'Something must be wrong with your hand, because you're just holding mine. Is yours hurt or something?'"

Dwight released his hand from Steve's and glanced at it.

"'Nothing's wrong with my hand,' I said. 'I just didn't want to squeeze yours.' This somehow triggered the guy. He must have thought I was trying to insult his white manhood or something, or maybe he was trying to impress his girlfriend."

Gruff silence ensued, during which Steve made no attempt to engage in further conversation of any kind with Dwight.

Dwight's well-appointed bedroom was equipped for a student. Ample lighting, a desk for study, a separate air conditioner, and even a stereo record player were available to him. "These were things I expected I'd find in a white home. And the bed was big and comfortable. A couple days into my visit, I even found that Mrs. Beltran had cleaned my room and remade my bed. The linen had been changed, although the beautiful spread that had been on the bed was now gone. The new sheets appeared a little dingy, but clean. A few days later, the spread reappeared, newly cleaned. She had changed the sheets again as well, and these were a little whiter. As far as I could see, the sheets and linens were all on the level. I assumed that the rotation of those things was a normal procedure."

Food could have been an issue as well, since Dwight learned early on in his visit that the meals emanating from a "white" kitchen were different from those from a "black" kitchen. "Mrs. Beltran always prepared a good hearty meal, which I never missed. She usually cooked 'white' food, like roast beef, ground beef, and some combinations of vegetables and meat together. I ate it all."

An issue of politesse and house procedure also came up for Dwight, i.e. who was to do the kitchen clean up? "After dinner, Mrs. Beltran always cleared the table and washed the dishes. I was shocked to know that the white mother of the house did this; after all, there were two other grownups there."

Eventually, the mysterious son did show up.

"He joined us for dinner, and was quiet and distant. I told him right away that I was sorry to inconvenience him by taking his room. He replied that it was all right. He liked sleeping in the den sometimes, he said."

There was nonetheless a problem. Dwight had had the bedroom entirely to himself when Pauline's brother was not in the house. But with his arrival, the expectations of one of the house's other occupants changed, and the change very much affected Dwight's comfort level.

"That night, I had to use the bathroom, and when I returned, I found the Doberman Pinscher asleep on the bed. I didn't know what to do. Then I thought I would play a trick on the dog. I tiptoed downstairs about halfway, and called to the dog lightly. The beast awoke and came to me. I was scared, but I didn't run. He barked and growled like hell, and the barking woke up the entire household."

Mr. Beltran arrived in his pajamas and led the Doberman away by the collar. He apologized, explaining that the dog customarily slept in the bedroom when their son was at home.

A restrained confrontation took place the next day. It seemed obvious to Dwight that Pauline's brother resented the imposition of a stranger on his own bedroom, and that he did not like being expelled to the den. Dwight of course wondered how much his being a black man sharpened the young man's unhappiness. The confrontation became clear the morning after Dwight's luring of the Doberman from the bedroom.

"I went downstairs, and from the bottom of the stairs I heard a growl. It was the dog, of course, whom I had privately named 'Satan.' He was in the den with Pauline's brother, who, it was now quite clear to me, was his master. Her brother said something to the effect that I shouldn't be coming downstairs so early. He didn't say it rudely…but I still didn't like it."

The silence between the two young men continued. "He remained a distant type of guy," Dwight writes in his journal. "He never stayed home very much. He went to school, and I learned that he worked for a veterinarian and played the piano quite well. Above all, he loved dogs."

Dwight made efforts to ingratiate himself further with the family, chipping in with chores and conversation whenever he could. But Pauline's brother remained distant. When he spoke, the words were merely muttered and for the most part monosyllabic, even dismissive. Dwight felt that he had made progress with everyone in the family except the Beltrans' son, and he decided that trying to get the young man to speak with him openly was a pointless endeavor.

But then, Dwight learned something about young Beltran that interested him and allowed for an opening in their relationship.

"He was a body builder, his sister told me. He liked working out. I liked that too. So I started talking to him about it…and he responded. I issued a challenge…and he accepted. We went to the gym together, and lifted. From then on, we got along fine. He respected me more after that."

One of the other surprises for Dwight in his home visit came from the father, Mr. Beltran himself. Dwight began the home visit worried that Mr. Beltran, being a white man, could possibly be a significant element in the visit's ultimate failure. "But getting to know him was no problem at all. He helped me with my homework!" Dwight worried out loud one night at dinner that he was contemplating dropping out of the university for a while. A few of the classes were more than he had anticipated, and he was concerned that he may not be up to them. "Mr. Beltran showed concern for me," Dwight wrote in his journal. "That I not quit. He proved to be especially helpful with my chemistry homework, which was really my big problem."

As the home visit continued through the week, everyone settled into routines that now included Dwight. They continued talking. He and Pauline's brother went to the gym. Dwight helped with the dishes and turned himself with new enthusiasm to his homework. And for him, the largest surprise was the affection the family showed him on his last day in their home.

"I felt very touched as I was walking out the front door of the Beltrans' house. Mr. Beltran addressed me, offered me his hand, and gave me a long handshake. What shocked me the most…something I could not have imagined just a week before…was that Mrs. Beltran and Pauline, white women both, two generations of white women, gave me hugs around my neck."

———

In 1973, Jim, a white student in Pete's class, was twenty-eight years old, an undergraduate major in political science at UNF. His journal reveals two items that placed him in a particular demographic that would be familiar to anyone who was a university student in the United States in the early 1970s.

For one, he had a long ponytail. Thus, one can guess, he was something of a hippie, or at least thought of himself as one. That movement, which since has been written about exhaustively, was particularly notable for its devoted white adherents nationwide and their discoveries in the use of psychedelic and other drugs, their adherence to Thoreau's notions of civil disobedience, their interest in the contemporary writing of the time like *The Making of A Counter Culture* by Theodore Roszak, *One Flew Over The Cuckoo's Nest* by Ken Kesey, *The Electric Kool-Aid Acid Test* by Tom Wolfe, and the most influential of them all, *The Greening of America* by Charles A. Reich. The hippie movement brought a fundamental change to much of the thinking in the western world about personal liberation and emotional discovery.

A political movement in the early 1970s that also affected the lives of many young people was embodied in the farmworkers' strike led by César Chávez's United Farmworkers Union in California. This complicated and contentious union struggle with the agriculture industry in that state has been described in many books and films. The most visible manifestations of the union's activities at the time were the five-year-long Delano grape strike that began in 1965 and the iceberg lettuce boycotts of the early 1970s. These two events brought the work and pay difficulties of immigrant California farmworkers to national attention, and the grape and lettuce boycotts had devoted adherents on college campuses throughout the United States.

In his journal, Jim mentions that he is involved with the lettuce boycott and that he has to pay attention to his volunteerism while at the same time not wishing to miss any session of the Human Conflict class. "Saturday I spent the morning getting the lettuce boycott underway."

Jim's political tendencies were to change, as we will see in the chapter entitled "Truth, Considered," later in this book. But at the time of his involvement with the Human Conflict class, he was involved enough in left-leaning politics to qualify as a liberal.

But Jim did have a very real, palpable prejudice against black people on his first day in the class. A few weeks in, he wrote this in his journal: "I was not aware of how deeply rooted my racial prejudices were. It is a struggle for me to come to terms with this problem, and to even admit that I had such a severe problem. There have been a couple of times when I felt like saying 'to hell with it' and getting out."

But Jim didn't get out, and perhaps the most telling anecdotes from his experience come in his account of the home visit.

Local high school baseball mattered to Leonard and Maxine, with whom Jim was to stay. One of the first things Jim learned when he arrived at their home in a black Jacksonville neighborhood was that the whole family would be attending a game at the local park, after church on the following Sunday. Jim was a baseball nut as well, and he sensed that this game would be different from any he had ever seen, simply because he had attended games all his life in which the teams and the fans were almost exclusively white people. He knew something about the famous Negro leagues...Josh Gibson, Satchel Paige, Cool Papa Bell, et. al....but by 1973 the major and minor professional leagues were integrated, and the Negro leagues no longer existed. What Branch Rickey, Jackie Robinson, and the Brooklyn Dodgers had succeeded in doing in 1947, when Robinson became the first black player to be signed to a major league team, had sounded the death knell of the Negro leagues. So, a laudable and necessary social change had ruined a formidably important cultural institution. Black people understood this, and naturally preferred what Robinson and all the other black players had done to affect the racial makeup of the professional teams and, by extension, the entire country.

But local black high school ball was still a big deal. So, Jim had a lot to look forward to on this coming Sunday.

First, he had to meet his hosts. He had only once visited a black neighborhood. Previous to that, his entire experience was that of driving through such a section of town when it provided the most efficient way of getting from one white neighborhood to another. The single actual experience in a black home that he did have, had taken place just two days before he was scheduled to begin his Human Conflict class home visit. One of the black students in the class had invited all the other students to her home for a soul food dinner.

Jim describes being greeted outside the home by one of his black classmates, Andrew, who invited him to take a walk around the neighborhood. "The first people we saw were two young black boys about ten or twelve years old. They stopped talking, and stared at us. Further down the block, we saw several young Blacks, male and female. They stopped talking, and stared at us. I felt hostility and careful scrutiny from these people."

Jim had never eaten soul food. He had only heard of it, an admission that, when he made it in class, brought loud laughter and comic castigation from all the black students. When he and Andrew entered the home for the dinner celebration, he was greeted by the others and escorted into the kitchen, where a large table was covered with platters of food...chicken fried steak, fatback, collard greens, black-eyed peas, okra, sweet potato pie, corn bread…. Jim writes in his journal that his favorite was the baked raccoon. He had not understood, prior to this evening, that raccoon was edible.

The dinner lasted several hours, during which much conversational back and forth between all the students broke whatever ice may still have existed between them after their few weeks in class. He writes in his journal that the next day, Friday, was recovery day—"from stuffing myself"—and preparing to introduce himself to Leonard and Maxine.

They lived in a neighborhood that, until a few years before, had been all white. As with many such neighborhoods, once a black family moved in, white families panicked and could be convinced by opportunistic real estate sales people to sell their properties. The neighborhood would quickly change, and become all black. Jim worried that, although Leonard and Maxine had agreed to host him, their neighbors may not be so welcoming. "My feelings lay somewhere between nervous and scared. 'Uncertain' would probably describe them best."

Maxine greeted Jim when he arrived in his car. Helping him with his things, she brought him into their home and showed him the room in which he would be staying. His initial surprise was that this home was rather like the one he had just left. It was middle-class, furnished tastefully in a comfortable way, with a garden and tended back yard. Maxine informed him that they were going to have dinner that evening with her mother, Miss Dolly, and Aunt Gussy, Miss Dolly's sister.

Leonard had preceded them to Miss Dolly's. When they arrived there, the front door flew open and a little girl came running out to the driveway. This was Maxine and Leonard's daughter Corinne who, the moment she spotted Jim, stopped cold and stared at the white man getting out of the car.

Maxine greeted her and explained that Jim was going to be living with them for a week, to which Corinne replied with a look that Jim describes as "amazement." "Why is a white boy going to live with us?" There was no hostility in the girl's utterance; simply surprise. No such thing had ever happened to her.

"The next person I met was Miss Dolly." Jim worried that, if she were displeased or made uncomfortable by this white stranger's arrival in her home, the entire home visit could be jeopardized. "I was feeling confused, and couldn't get my bearings. I tried to clear my head a bit, worried about how she would greet me." Miss Dolly extended her hand and welcomed Jim. She was immediately friendly, and invited him into the house. Miss Gussy's greeting was not as warm. "She was a little skeptical of the whole thing," Jim writes. "She would reserve judgment until later."

After a few minutes inside Miss Dolly's home, Jim met Leonard who, a moment later, took Jim aside for a private moment.

"Anything I can do?" he said.

Jim remained silent, still feeling ungainly and not knowing what to say.

"Listen, Jim, you can be sure that, if this situation were reversed, I'd feel pretty strange too."

"I felt like hugging him for this unexpected kindness," Jim writes.

Dinner was filled with conversation, mostly about school and Jim's classes. When the Human Conflict class finally came up, everyone expressed surprise that it existed at all. That no one had ever suggested such a curriculum made sense to everyone, given the history of the region during the past few hundred years. And now, the newness of it, the very idea of it, was cause around the table for the appreciative laughter that accompanies an unusual surprise, and questions of Jim from everyone about what was going on in the class. When he described the confrontational nature of some of the conversations in class, a variety of opinions came from the others around the table, from the sort that expressed great caution about what could be uncovered, to those that were congratulatory of the argument and the straightforward subject material that was being handled so openly. Revelation followed upon revelation, sometimes with worry from those listening, other times with actual amazement. Jim himself was by no means the only source of surprise. He especially was taken aback by the very strong emotions that he could feel from everyone. Not all the emotions were positive...sometimes what he was describing brought a sense of apprehension from someone else at the table. What someone else still felt about what had happened fifty years earlier to a friend of the family or relative, chagrined Jim himself, something that person had not survived either emotionally or in fact. Jim learned more of what he had been learning in class, about the daily and constant difficulties of being a black person, as well as about the determination of Blacks to build a reputation, a profession, and an actual life despite such troubles.

After dinner, Miss Dolly asked Jim to join her at the local food market. "I want to show you off," she said. He accompanied her, once again made nervous by his fear of the possible reaction of other customers at the store. To his surprise, the first person to whom Miss Dolly introduced him was her husband, Maxine's father, named Snoop. He explained that he had had to work and, so, couldn't make it to dinner. He turned to the two men with whom he had been talking before Jim's arrival in the conversation, and introduced them as his two brothers. They too wanted to know about the dinner, and what this home visit thing was all about. They were interested… very interested. They had never heard of anything like this before.

The following Sunday, Jim went to church. He wasn't sure what to expect. He suspected that the parishioners would be surprised by his appearance in their place of worship, and indeed they were. But the surprise was even greater for Jim.

He was already a regular churchgoer, in a white establishment in his own neighborhood. He describes his place of worship as being a comfortable building in which "everything was expensive and new." That building itself was just a few years old. Its furniture and pews were well made and kept up by a paid staff, waxed and polished. Everything was painted, everything cared for. One wouldn't see a scratched wall or scuffed floors. The rugs, though spartan in their decoration, were very clean. This was a place of repose and quiet, everything so well tended that, when it was empty, the place seemed hardly used. This misconception was corrected on Sundays, when Jim's church was filled with devout, prayerful, charitable, and kindly people, all white.

Jim escorted Miss Dolly into the Reverend Roberson's small church. It was a clapboard building, painted white, situated in the middle of a plain of grass a few yards from the street that ran before it. The building had been here for a while, and was in no way well to do. It was cared for, but plain, with little of the luxury of Jim's own church. Other parishioners were arriving, and all were well dressed. The men wore suits and ties (as did Jim, by the way, his pony tail securely gathered in a rubber band, and combed by him carefully so that it would not appear unruly or disrespectful.) The children were similarly formal in their attire. The boys wore coats and ties, like their fathers and other relatives. The girls were formal in colorful dresses, with short white socks and Mary Janes, their hair carefully done by their mothers. The women were dressed in clothing that bespoke respect for the occasion. Many were wearing the fully adorned hats for which black church-going women are often noted. Like a symbol for thoughtful, yet celebratory, Christian self-regard, these hats flower Sunday celebrations in the black church.

It was a sunny, warm morning, and a jovial gathering of parishioners was moving up the cement pathway toward the church building's front doors. The greetings were friendly. Clasped hands in greeting and the clapping of backs. Big hugs and laughter among the women. People were glad to be here. Jim sensed the fellow feeling that these people had for each other and—despite their obvious curiosity—for him. He was greeted and welcomed, most especially during the service when almost the first thing that Reverend Roberson uttered as he began his sermon was a warm welcome to their guest, the gentleman sitting with Miss Dolly and her family. He invited Jim to return to his church any time he wished.

The church interior was quite plain. It had a wood floor and wooden pews…more benches than pews, actually, with backs. Folding metal chairs as well, to accommodate late-comers or stragglers. The church was full.

Jim describes Reverend Roberson's sermon. "His service was different from white churches. After reading from Scripture, he began preaching. He spoke with ever-increasing rhythm. It became almost hypnotic. He kept exhorting the deacons and the congregation to 'talk to me, talk to me.'" Jim felt himself enthralled by the reverend's voice and his thorough command of verse, chapter, and biblical reference. The parishioners were paying close attention, and answering out loud, frequently, with affirmations of what Reverend Roberson was quoting and occasional replies that contained bits of Scripture also applicable to what he was saying. His exhortations frequently brought laughter and affirmation from the parishioners. There was of course also music, provided by a single standup piano played by an older woman, and a choir of about a dozen parishioners, men and women. Jim remarked the joy of all this, so different from the quiet and careful decorum of the white church that he attended regularly.

Afterward, he was escorted by some of the parishioners to the adjoining cemetery, who gave Jim the history of the church and an assessment of what it meant to them and their families to have this place and to have Reverend and Mrs. Roberson here to counsel them and to help them when help was needed. They pointed to this or that gravestone, describing for Jim an uncle who laid beneath this one, a sister or a mother who lay beneath that.

"The remainder of our time there was spent discussing racial problems and the ideas we each had about what could be done to ease those problems." This conversation had none of the raucous back and forth that those in the Human Conflict class provided. "We didn't come to any fantastic solutions," Jim writes. "But at least we were talking, and they wanted to talk with me."

Jim returned to Leonard and Maxine's home, and everyone changed to more casual clothes. It was time for some baseball.

The family drove to a local park, where a tended, chalk-marked diamond was bordered on the first- and third-base sides by open-air wooden bleachers, enough to hold a crowd of a few hundred. There were no dugouts; rather long benches behind the high cyclone fence that protected the crowd from errant foul balls. Each uniformed team would occupy these benches when they were off the field. Bats lay on the ground or were leaned up against the fence. The sharp snap of balls against gloves accompanied the chatter between the uniformed players as they warmed up. The bleachers filled. Fans of each team occupied the opposite sets of bleachers.

Jim was the one white person in the crowd. "I noticed that I did stay real close to Leonard while we were at the ball game," he writes. "I guess I was more worried than I had thought I would be at first."

But here too, the attitude of the Blacks sitting everywhere around Jim was friendly. He noticed how many of the fans would look toward him, and that there would be occasional snippets of conversation between them about his presence at the game. A woman would point Jim out, surreptitiously, to her husband, who then a moment later would glance at him. A couple of young boys sitting with their parents would stare at him, trying to figure him out. An old man would spot him and look away, shaking his head. Leonard and Maxine introduced Jim to several people seated nearby, and as the game progressed, he was engaged in conversation. "I was the oddity," he writes.

At the beginning of the game, Jim realized that there was indeed one other oddity. "The opposing team's pitcher...he was white too. The *only* other White. And as he was taking his first inning warm-ups, I found myself, instead of identifying with him, looking at him in much the same light as the other spectators: that is, as an anachronism."

—

It would be comfortable to describe only those home visits that went well, in which all the student participants came to cherish the wonderful treatment they were getting from the hosts, and vice versa. But that would be an untruth. In some cases, the gulf between Blacks and Whites remained for the participants throughout the visit, and afterwards. The reports from these kinds of visits usually express the original wish, by both sides, to cross the gap between the two races. But sometimes the gap is just too broad, and the initial sincerity collapses into, at best, indifference or, at worst, deepened hostility. One such is the home visit of a black student named Alfonso.

Alfonso encountered a specific difficulty the moment he entered the class on the first day. "I was a little disappointed because I had pictured the instructor as being black. After hearing the requirements for the class, I was left wondering what this guy Kranz was up to."

The idea of the home visit was okay with Alfonso, although he noticed that, after a few weeks of the class, he was the only Black left who had not yet been assigned a visit. Apparently he did not ask about this, and no explanation was given to him. Finally, after three weeks, he was assigned to spend the week in the home of a UNF professor and his wife, whom I will name Mr. and Mrs. Dudley.

While awaiting the assignment, Alfonso pondered the possibilities. He had already been put off by Pete Kranz's being white. The delay in the home visit assignment put him off even more, since it seemed to Alfonso that he was being intentionally held back for some unknown reason. "So, before the visit, I came up with the idea of just writing some bullshit in my journal…you know, a fiction…and not even staying with the Dudleys. I knew that living with them and just lying to them all the time wouldn't work. When I'm at home, I hardly say ten words to my own parents, and now, what am I going to say, or want to say, to the Dudleys?"

The first day of the visit is usually one for introductions, a tour through the home, the visitor's bedroom, how to get to the bathroom…etc. These are the most every-day of moments, the first of the feeling-out process that eventually will bring the visitor into the household, hopefully confident of being welcomed. The home sponsors, of course, are just as concerned that their own interests not be jeopardized. Usually they are asking one of their kids to move into a den or a playroom or some such, so that the visitor can have privacy. It's a moment important to the success—or failure— of the visit.

Alfonso's first contact with the Dudleys was his phone call the afternoon of the first day of his visit.

"Hello Mrs. Dudley, this is Alfonso, from Dr. Kranz's class?"

"Hello, Alfonso. How are you?"

"I'm okay, but I won't be able to get there tonight until somewhere between 7:30 and 9:30."

"Oh…I see. Is there a problem?"

"No, it's just that I've got something to do."

"What's that?"

"Just…something. It's important."

After a pause, Mrs. Dudley said that she understood, but that Alfonso would miss dinner. Alfonso nodded to himself, knowing that that was exactly the outcome he was seeking. He finally did arrive, at 8:30, in the company of his two roommates, both black UNF students. They had driven him to the Dudleys', and Alfonso does not explain in his journal whether they were there to bolster his confidence, to provide a reason for not staying at all, to check out the territory that Alfonso was being forced to enter… whatever.

Alfonso decided to stay. After his roommates left, he sat down to a warmed up dinner and, finally, engaged Professor and Mrs. Dudley in conversation. "It lasted pretty late. I gathered that Mrs. Dudley was the one who had decided that I would stay with them. Mr. Dudley seems like a guy that lets his wife have what she wants. Mrs. Dudley was nice, except she talks too much."

The second night's dinner was different. There was more conversation, during which Alfonso learned a bit more about Professor Dudley. It was information delivered apparently without enthusiasm by the professor. I include Alfonso's journal description of the meal here in its entirety.

"Mr. Dudley didn't get home from the university until 5:30 p.m. He asked me why we had to stay in a white home, and Whites in a black home. I said that the class was about racial conflict. He asked who our instructor was and what he was like. Mr. Dudley then commented that you can't intend to accomplish too much with just a one-week visit. From this statement, I began to wonder where Mr. Dudley's head was. I replied that the only way to get into it is for me to be with you, and that maybe both of us would find differences in the way we feel about the opposite race. We really began to talk then, even with a little harshness, until we began to talk about our families. Mr. Dudley asked if I had any siblings. 'Sure, I have four sisters and one brother, and my parents are divorced and both are remarried.' After that particular statement, Mrs. Dudley seemed as though she thought I was going through some emotional stress about my parents. Mr. Dudley didn't want to talk any more. We didn't get into any more heavy discussion during my visit."

Apparently from this moment forward, the home visit had little effect upon the three participants. Alfonso writes that he did nothing to change his personal style from anything he would usually do. He ate dinner with his baseball cap on, and apparently no one asked him to remove it. They spoke very little. If Mrs. Dudley cooked something that Alfonso did not like, he didn't eat it, and did not comment on it. If he didn't like how it looked when it was served, he wouldn't taste it.

The Dudleys watched educational television programs, to which Alfonso voiced his displeasure. To his surprise, the Dudleys then let him watch what he wished, although they would leave the room.

Alfonso's last entry in his journal records the following: "I like Mrs. Dudley, but she scares the shit out of me every morning that she drives me to school. I have uneasy feelings around Professor Dudley."

———

Another less-than-successful home visit involved Lee, a white woman, and her home hosts Mary and Lawrence. After the completion of her week in their home, Lee waited for some days before describing the experience in her journal. She admits that she has been having trouble gathering her thoughts. But her reaction to the home visit is clear. "I don't think I will ever see Mary and Lawrence again. They certainly will not call me, and I don't have a reason to call them."

Lee says that, early in her home visit, she made efforts at communication that were rebuffed by both her hosts. She wanted to talk, but worried that her way of conversation ("Sometimes I am quick to state an opinion before I have really felt the true effect of a situation.") was off-putting to both hosts. Both seemed to her indifferent, even uncaring, about this process through which they all were going. "I went to their house expecting miracles, and nothing happened." Finally, after a few nights, she asked Lawrence in front of some acquaintances of his and Mary (all black people) if he couldn't find a way to talk with her more openly about the racial issues that were being discussed in class. "He let loose with a wave of hatred that was unbelievable," Lee writes. "Since there were strangers in the room whom I did not know, I was hesitant to speak up for myself. I didn't know how hostile Blacks in general could be toward me, and I felt uncomfortable."

Lawrence was having none of it. In a strident voice, he dressed Lee down summarily. "If he could only speak in a natural, calm voice, it would be easier to communicate with him." But he would not calm down, and we find out later, from a further entry in Lee's journal, that Lawrence's hostility toward her was always immediate, very real, and easily sparked. "He either shuts up, or goes on for hours," she writes.

Mary too was hostile toward Lee, but expressed her anger in a very different way. Silence or, at best, few words were the most she would offer. "Mary went the whole time with an attitude of apathy. She did not care about my being there, and said that she did not have time to get into a deep discussion. I did try, but we only skimmed the surface of any discussion of racial fears. For example, I told her once that I was afraid when a car filled with black men would drive by me. Her response was that she had heard that before. Nothing else. 'Yeah, I've heard that before.'"

What is not known in this account of Lee's home visit is the source of Lawrence and Mary's hostility. One can speculate…that something in Lee's personality was irritating to them or abrasive of them, or that Lawrence and Mary felt that this whole experiment of the Human Conflict class was foolish, or that Lee and/or Mary and Lawrence were driven by racist antipathy, white against black, black against white, or that Lee was so incapable of understanding the racial situation that she was simply unreachable…so why try? Any number of other possible explanations.

Lawrence and Mary did not have the opportunity that Lee had in her journal, to explain their feelings. So, sadly, we can't know specifically and plainly why that home visit was for them such a failure.

—

In a later interview, one black female student described her feelings before embarking on her own home visit. "I was very, very apprehensive, even up to the very point of the day when I was supposed to go. I really thought that I didn't want to go. I decided that I would use my son as an excuse, so that if it wasn't working out, I could easily say, 'Well, I have to go home.' I am outspoken, but I really felt, that day, very vulnerable going into a white home. I did not have a support system. I didn't have the backing of the few friends I had from the class. I had no parental system to help me."

Things changed for her after the first day of her visit. "They were a family, a working family with school children. They hustled. They bustled. They had their little family times together and their disagreements.

Nobody's perfect, but this was good. To see a white family [like I did] as they really exist is almost impossible. It was great."

—

There is a home visit the result of which actually saved the class for one white student. Karen was staying with Dr. and Mrs. Appleton. (Dr. Appleton was a pediatrician.) She was having such trouble in class one day that she broke down and wept in front of all the others. Blacks and Whites were getting after her for a few things that she was trying to explain about herself. Interruptions came, along with caustic accusations of insincerity and wrong thinking. "It was as though the ceiling fell in on me. When I went home to the Appletons, I told Mrs. Appleton about it and began to cry again. She was very much a mother figure. She just held me and rocked me. It was just like her own daughter had come in weeping. I was so glad I was staying with them, rather than having gone back to my own apartment, where I lived alone."

—

A home visit that seemed to get off on the wrong foot initially becomes one of the most successful...if it can be said that the calm understanding of real, and fixed, differences of opinion is a form of success. In the case of Luther, who was to spend his home visit with a white couple named Edward and Winona, Luther's initial understanding of his host's racial politics was not a happy one. "Edward doesn't have any special liking for black people," Luther writes. "He doesn't like the way we walk, the way we talk. The only things he admires about us is the way we dance and the way we dress."

Originally, Luther learned this about Edward because they had the unusual circumstance of both being students in the same Human Conflict class. Usually a student would have a home visit with someone not taking the class. In this case, both men knew each other on a weekly basis in the classroom. During the home visit, they were also living together, the black student in the white student's home.

At first, Luther was reluctant. He knew how Edward felt about black people because Edward had told him so, along with the rest of the class, on the first day, in response to Pete Kranz's question, "Why did you sign up for this class?"

In an interview with Luther some years later, he explored the nature of his understanding of Whites before he was to arrive at UNF. "I graduated from all-black Stanton High School. It was founded in 1868, and named for Edwin Stanton, who was Abraham Lincoln's Secretary of War. It was the first public school for black children in the state of Florida. Before I got to UNF, I had very little contact with white people. There were white merchants and vendors in my neighborhood: laundrymen, insurance people, and so on, who were friendly to us. But of course we *were* their bread and butter."

Luther's feelings about white people in general can be discerned in a story he told in this same interview, about his job as a bag boy in a grocery store when he was in high school. "I was trying to bag this white guy's purchases, when he grabbed the bag out of my hand and huffed, 'You people, you're trying to take everything over.'"

"America has always had a history of blaming minorities when times are bad," Luther explained in the interview. "It's bad enough that, even with all our achievements and qualifications, we Blacks are still either the last hired and first fired, or are those doing the same work as our white counterparts, while getting paid less for it. This is not always the case, but in most instances, it is."

Luther's early treatment of Edward in class also came up during this interview. "The class we were in was so unequal in number that two or three Blacks were sometimes put together with one White. By the time we got raw and told this poor guy Edward about what we thought about white people, I felt kind of sorry for him. Sure, we were saying things that he needed to hear, but he was getting it in two's and three's. When he told us about his dislike of Blacks, we countered with things that I guess...." Luther did not finish the sentence.

It then became time for Luther to go on his home visit with Edward. "I showed my fright, I guess, in my procrastination," Luther says in his journal, "I kept putting off going [to Edward's house.] I kept wanting to stay in my comfortable womb. I stayed away at least until Wednesday of the week I was supposed to be doing the home visit." Luther thought about it, cogitated, and waited. "But I knew I had to cut the umbilical cord, and venture out into the white world to see what was there."

Luther had gotten a last-minute insight into Edward's attitudes toward black people a week before, once Edward had completed his own visit to a black family's home. He had regaled his classmates with a description of it that signaled a distinct change in Edward's feelings. "He shocked the whole class," Luther writes in his journal. "He is definitely a changed Edward, no doubt about it. That dude's negative attitudes toward Blacks had been unbelievable, although at least he was honest enough to come to grips with it [in front of us]. He still has some growing to do, but, boy! has he made strides! I must admit that he is more open with his feelings now."

Luther got into his car early that Wednesday morning and set out for Edward's place. "I got lost. Probably hoping unconsciously that I wouldn't find it. But I knew I couldn't turn back. After more wrong turns and misguided miles, I arrived."

Luther got his things out of the back seat of his car and walked up the stairs to the front door of Edward's apartmen, ringing the bell. "Edward greeted me. He was as uncomfortable as I was." Edward motioned Luther into the apartment, into the living room. "I stood for about five minutes," Luther writes, "until he finally asked me to sit down." One thing particularly that Luther noticed was the quantity and, he thought, quality of the paintings that were hanging from the living room walls. Edward admitted that he was the artist, that painting was an avocation of his. Luther notes in his journal that Edward's work is "pretty good... 'impressionistic' landscapes."

Luther felt there were plusses and minuses to be found in the apartment. "The books, the paintings...the orderliness!...impressed me. But the dog and the two cats didn't. How can people and animals subsist in such a close environment? Ugh! It disgusted me: the animal odor, the shed hair all over the place."

Discomfort between the two men continued for several minutes, until

Edward finally began a conversation. There is no record in either man's journal of what subjects the conversation covered, but it does not sound like the *tête-à-tête* was a very successful one. "There was more silence than anything else," Luther says. After a half hour or so of disjointed exchange, Edward stood, announcing that he had a twelve o'clock class at UNF, and that he didn't want to be late. "I was relieved when he left, in a way. I really wanted to take a nap, and didn't want to appear just unfriendly."

Edward had showed Luther where his bedroom was, and he took up his things. Walking up the hallway toward the room, he noticed the dog and one of the cats following him. "They marched in behind me. I was horrified when I thought of sleeping in that room with those animals. The only thing I could think of was going to sleep, and then being awakened by the cat walking across my chest." Luther dropped his gear to the floor and looked about the room, not sure how he was going to handle this crisis so soon after his arrival, and without the host to help him with it. "But the animals excused themselves from the room. Boy, was I relieved! I closed the door and went to sleep."

The seeming light comedy of this situation devolves into a further predicament a few hours later that, for Luther, was anything but funny. "I got up at two thirty, to get ready to go to the school myself. But I found that there was no way to lock the front door to the apartment from the outside without a key, and I had no key. This meant that I had to wait for Edward to get home. He didn't get home until three-fifteen, which meant that I had already missed the beginning of my class."

Edward was apologetic, and told Luther that he could have left the door unlocked. But Luther insisted that he couldn't do such a thing. Fresh in his mind, and kept to himself by Luther, had been Edward's story from their conversation earlier that two of the apartments in the complex had been broken into recently. "The thing that kept going through my mind was that, if I had left that door open, and someone had broken into the apartment, there would have been no possible way to convince the police that I did not conspire to rob Edward's apartment."

He ends the paragraph in which he has been describing his predicament: "Race relations in Jacksonville just aren't that good yet."

Given some of the general distrustful assumptions on the part of local Whites about black people (mentioned in many of the white students' descriptions of how they were raised, and their parents' attitudes toward Blacks), it makes sense that Luther would be fearful of how such a break-in to Edward's apartment could be viewed by Edward and the all-white Jacksonville police force. But Edward, in his own journal of a day or so later, expresses a surprising opinion: "Luther wouldn't leave the apartment unlocked until I got home. He missed part of his class, and I felt badly about it. I'm sure that many people would have simply left the door unlocked...but not Luther."

Luther had not yet met Edward's wife Winona. He knew she worked at the public library in Jacksonville, and had once been a public school teacher. He describes his own knowledge of the library and his wondering if, among all the white women who worked there, he has ever met Winona. Returning from class (he had succeeded in making it to the second half of it), he walked up the stairs to Edward's apartment and, still without a key, knocked on the door. Edward answered and stepped back from the door, gesturing Luther in. Winona stood behind Edward, and did not wait to be introduced. She came forward offering her hand. The three of them talked for several minutes, about the class, about the home visit idea, and other things. Finally, Winona excused herself and went into the kitchen to continue preparing the dinner meal. It was simple...spaghetti and a salad, delicious in Luther's opinion.

"After dinner, Edward and I started in on a game of Scrabble. It was my first time playing. Needless to say, I lost." This loss, however, brought about an opening in the conversation that was to continue for the rest of Luther's home visit. "I think I surprised Edward with my choice of words, and my quickness to challenge what seemed like made-up words." There was considerable kidding and laughter.

Edward's journal entry about that same day is more detailed than is Luther's, and it gives the reader a chance to see a softening in both men's attitudes toward each other. Edward's respect for Luther grows, especially when Luther shows him a particular book that he has brought back with him from school. Here are some of Edward's observations:

"Luther doesn't like to cut loose with deep feelings. He keeps his distance. He communicates well, is knowledgeable and intelligent. But he maintains an invisible shield…an inability, perhaps, to be intimate."

This may be a lot to ask of Luther after only a day or so of the home visit, especially in view of Luther's recalling Edward's description of black people on the first day of class: the dancing, the way they dress, et. al. But when Luther comes back from class that day, Edward writes, he brings with him an illustrated book about art by black painters. Earlier in the day, when Luther had noted Edward's work, Edward explained that he had taken four art history courses in his college years. Thanking Luther for bringing the book with him, Edward, perusing it, mentioned that he had never heard of any of the artists whose work was in it. For that matter, he had never heard of any black artists at all. "But this stuff is damned good, exhibited in museums around the world!"

Luther nodded, and pointed to the book, tapping its front cover a couple times. Edward would soon read that book.

The discussion of art continued. "A friend of ours came over a little later that afternoon," Edward writes. "He's a long-haired 'hippie-commie', a photographer who wanted to take some black and white pictures of all of us. He told us a lot about shutter speeds, f-stops, super X film, Polaroids, etc. etc." The conversation continued through dinner, until the beginning of the Scrabble game between Edward and Luther. "I beat him," Edward writes. "It was his first game of Scrabble, and he gave me a hard time about it."

That conversation continued into the evening. Luther's reticence continued, but Edward's own resistance to the situation softened. "Luther seems to me like an oyster with a pearl inside it. Dr. Kranz gets on him in class…about his performance in class, his quiet. But working a midnight shift and going to school is no joke. I have a lot of respect for him, since his scholastic performance is greatly hindered by extremely adverse conditions. He's willing to stick it out.

"After the Scrabble game, I asked Luther if he thought staying with us would help him. He said that he thought it would since he thinks the white life-style is so different from that of the black community. More serene. Less excitement. He said he had suspected that, and had wanted to see it."

Edward had one more task for that evening, which was to continue writing a paper for one of his classes at UNF. He intended to share it with the Human Conflict class first. He showed Luther the draft of what he had done so far. Luther took it in hand. "I was worried about what he would say," Edward says. "For me, the technical aspect of writing is like learning to read music. It only gets in the way." After a moment, Luther took a pencil to Edward's manuscript. He found flaws, enough of them to impress Edward with what he knew about how to write. Good spelling, proper sentence structure, correct grammar.... Those are the things Edward worried about when he thought of "the technical aspect" of writing, and Luther was able to help him. "I needed to start the paper over," Edward writes, and he was glad to do so.

The paper's theme was that white America had lied to Edward and, in so doing, had made a racist of him. He had worried that he had not expressed this idea very well, especially the aspects of his upbringing that had resulted in his racism. He felt his own writing got in the way, thus impairing the authority that he wished to bring to his newfound understanding. His writing was hobbling him. "I think what counts is that I get my feelings across," he wrote in his journal. Luther's help with the writing brought Edward closer to that goal.

—

Michael H., a white student, was assigned to his home visit with Mrs. Bartley, a divorced black woman with five children. One of her kids was Debbie, who was also a student at UNF.

Debbie wanted Michael H. to meet a friend of hers, a black fellow student named George who was working on a Master's degree in Business at UNF. "She asked me to join them one night at 'The Lot,' and at first I didn't know what that was." Debbie pulled the car to the curb before a modest single story house in the same neighborhood in which the Bartleys lived. A very tall, slim young black man stood on the curb, and waved as the car approached. Michael H. noticed how stylishly this fellow was dressed, in the very cool fashions of a street-wise young black collegiate.

These clothes were quiet different from those Michael H. had on. Michael H. was wearing a short-sleeved paisley button-down shirt, a pair of khakis and brown penny loafers, the kind of clothing *de rigueur* at the time among his fellow middle-of-the-road white college students. But George was dressed in stylish black sweatpants, a dark blue T-shirt emblazoned with the words "Florida Gators" in bright orange, and white Adidas Superstar/ Americana basketball shoes. (Steve Williams, the first black player to be allowed onto the University of Florida's basketball team, was playing point guard for the Gators in 1972.) Despite it's being early evening, George wore black-rimmed sunglasses. His hair was done in an excessively neat, close-cropped Afro.

To Michael H.'s surprise, George engaged him and Debbie right away in a conversation about the lack of communication among the young people he knew, why people had so many "hang-ups," and why there was so much emphasis put on "false fronts", as George called them. George explained that he himself was a sometime basketball player, and that he often had to put up a front intended to soften everyone's expectations that, as tall as he was, he must be some kind of physical freak. He explained that he felt he had to be more somber and reflective-appearing than he really was, because he was so often kidded for his height. He wished to be looser in his own behavior—Michael H. had already noted that George was a genuinely humorous man—but his height made him feel that he should remain quiet and introspective-seeming. "Not a threat," he said. He also explained to Michael H. that, with some of his white acquaintances, he felt he had to be on the defense at all times. "I'm not sure I know how to take their friendship," he said.

Debbie and George took Michael H. to "The Lot," as it was called, the parking lot outside a store called Jax Liquors. There was a lounge next door as well. Basically a hangout for college-age black kids, The Lot was filled with automobiles on this evening, and Michael H. found that he was one of only a few white people there. The black men were dressed in styles similar to George's.

Michael H. was not comfortable.

"We decided to go into the lounge. While walking towards the entrance,

I heard, 'Hey, George, what are you doing with that white dude?'" Some of them gathered around the two men, laughing quietly and studying this new, comedic companion of George's. The tone of voice was mirthful and disrespecting, as though Michael H. were himself...paisley shirt, white-boy skin, and all... some kind of freak.

"At first I was hurt for myself and for the position that I had put Debbie and George into. Later, George tried to apologize for what had happened. I told him not to worry about it, that it didn't bother me, when in fact it had. Inside the lounge, I was worried about what the Blacks were thinking about me. I was used to being in the majority...i.e. white...and the idea of being a minority was very uncomfortable. When leaving we had to pass through a large group of black males again. My apprehension was nearly to a point of fear."

Michael H. got back into the car with George, Debbie at the wheel. Michael H. remained for the most part silent during the ride home. "I didn't admit to my fear. I didn't want to damage my ego, to admit to my stupidity. I wasn't sure how to handle it."

Debbie's mother Mrs. Bartley asked Michael H. one evening to accompany her to a Bible study class. Never having attended such a class in a black church, he joined her. There would be spoken readings from Scripture and discussions of what had been read.

"During the meeting I noticed that the very young and the very old people had to be helped with their readings. I would have expected this from the kids...some of them were only eight or nine years old. But it was obvious to me that the older people couldn't read because of a lack of education. I realized this had to be due to the restrictions placed on them by white control of the education system. I felt guilty. Older white people that I knew had no problems with reading.

Michael H. was to have one more experience at The Lot, when Debbie asked him once again to join her there.

"I thought about my earlier experience in the lounge, and considered trying to dress more to black standards than to my own. I was trying to make myself less obvious in black surroundings."

The folly of this idea became quickly obvious to Michael H. "I didn't like being in the minority. But I realized that Whites trying to fit themselves into a black situation would be no more help to any of us than Blacks trying to be white. Both must keep their identity, and accept the other simply for what that particular identity is."

Michael H. thought deeply about how he had felt at the lounge and what he had learned from it. The lessons were difficult for him, and he did not feel that he had absorbed them particularly well.

"I had known Blacks before this, and made them fit into my stereotype of what a Black should be. I never really accepted them as people. At times, I even used them as a kind of merit badge, making sure that everyone knew that I had black friends. So…I was using them for my own personal satisfaction. It took that week with Debbie and her family to make me realize this. And of course it also showed me my own prejudices…clearly…which up to that time I would never have admitted to. I had typed Blacks as either 'militants' or 'Uncle Toms.' But then I was admitted into Debbie's home better than I have been by some of the white people in the neighborhood where I live. After hearing of their personal experiences, and seeing the hardships and hurdles Blacks have had to face, I can't say that I blame them for hating Whites."

—

One of the most unusual home visits was that of Mike, who was the first white student to stay in the home of UNF's Director of Admissions, Ben, and his family, who were black. Mike was amused by the fact that he had a blonde pony-tail that extended to the middle of his back…a white hippy, which made him, he felt, even a little more unusual as a visitor to Ben's home than a more conventional (and uptight) white student would be.

As a child, Mike had had very direct witness of blatant racism, the memories of which remained with him into adulthood. "My dad once drove me past a Ku Klux Klan rally where there was a burning cross." The reflected light of the flames from the white robes of the Klansmen, and the odd feeling of great celebration that came from the rally, shocked the little boy. "And then I once saw a black man being denied entrance to a white church. I remember the preacher shaking his head at the man and pointing him back out toward the street." This too shocked the boy.

"I knew these things were wrong," Mike wrote in his UNF class journal. "And that as a white man, I had the luxury of tuning it out, [even though] through my childhood I had become somewhat aware of a world about which, really, I had remained nonetheless clueless. So that started me on a self-investigation."

Mike's joining Pete's class was a specific example of his wish to continue that investigation. But he already had significant experience with black people that most Whites in the South would not have been able, or willing, to entertain.

"I was raised in an all-white neighborhood, attended all-white schools, and went to an all-white church. My world was white and almost entirely Protestant. In junior college, and early in my time at UNF, I had a job working for a black church in an all-black neighborhood. Formerly the area had been all white, but the Whites had moved out as Blacks had moved in. The church board hired me to work with neighborhood children, and the only Whites were the pastor and me."

Mike's tenure in this position lasted for two years. The work had to do with Christian teachings and the early education of small children in the precepts and practices of Baptist Protestantism. His time here was very positive. "I had a youth program with over three hundred young people, and occasionally I would preach when the pastor was on vacation. I was treated very well by everyone."

Despite this positive relationship with that church's membership, Mike began his home visit with Ben and his family with some anxiety. The first few days of the Human Confrontation class, which for him were noted for the hostility between the Blacks and Whites, shocked him.

"Sometimes you felt you would literally attack someone…it was that intense. Really, I was a pacifist with long hair and a moustache. But in class, the Blacks treated me like I was a typical white racist. This was a real opening of my young mind. Before, as a kid and in the church, I had been trying to fit everyone into my own little shoebox."

As much as he cherished his work with the black church, Mike suddenly felt it to have been an enclosed experience…the shoebox…that had kept him from important truths. He had not gotten a complete view of how Blacks really felt about Whites. He had been shielded from such a view, probably, he thought, by the genuine care for him felt by the Blacks in the church; but also, Mike was to sense, by his own naivety and unwillingness to question the genuineness of the kindness being shown him by the parishioners. He did not feel that anyone there intentionally lied to him or tried to mislead him. He felt instead that the church members were probably applying their honest Christian beliefs to the situation in which they found themselves with this young, kind, naïve white boy. Mike had not learned yet what Price Cobbs had articulated in his writings…that race and its injustices are *always* issues for black people in the United States. For *every* black person.

But Blacks in the class were now showing him how that constancy of anger was a norm. "I was dealing with people who didn't fit the box," Mike wrote in his journal. "So I had to expand it, to accommodate them."

It was a strain for him. Mike endured the continued anger expressed toward him by black members of the class. "For them, I was just the stereotypical white guy. No matter how I expressed my previous experiences or my current attitudes…I was just a racist, like all other white guys." But the anger shown to Mike, in the end, produced in him new understandings to which, without the harassment by the Blacks in the class, he may never have come.

He realized that the intensity of that anger by no means put the lie to the kindness that he had observed in the church. It was just one other vibrant aspect of what it was like to be black. The kindness and the rage did not conflict with each other. They both were genuine. "Understanding that, my world has become a much bigger place than I could ever have imagined," he wrote in his journal.

When Ben showed Mike to the room in which he would be staying during the home visit, Mike realized that he would be sharing it with his hosts' two kids. The children were young, primary school students, part of an experiment during this week that perhaps they understood, perhaps not. Mike noticed how nonchalant Ben was when he explained that the two young ones were to have a roommate for a week. Mike wrote in his journal toward the end of the class: "Ben's family opened up and received me as though we were blood relatives. They put me in the same room with their two children. Here I was, hair down to my butt. I could have been a drug dealer, for all they knew. I was just overwhelmed by their acceptance. That was a sermon of trust."

Mike's youthful experience in the church continued deepening his sense of the values of the Christian religion, and furthered his interest in exploring it. After leaving UNF, he became involved with an international Christian organization that was hundreds of years old and very respected worldwide.

"After becoming an active member, I was nominated and elected as an officer of the organization, and I began doing regular public speaking events on their behalf. I was told that I had quite a future, and I was honored by the distinction that the organization offered me. But I quickly noticed, and then began to realize as I attended more meetings and did more work for them, that there were no black people in the organization. I was horrified, and the more I looked, the worse were my feelings for what I was witnessing.

"I approached the church leadership and confronted them…all white men. I was literally told, 'They have theirs, and we have ours.' I then wrote a long letter to the president of the international, in which I resigned my position: 'On no terms can I be a part of the practices that you espouse.' In the letter, I also cited biblical examples and passages of scripture that denounced segregationist practices. At the end of the letter, I offered the possibility of my returning to the organization, to be part of what I saw were needed changes, if and when they decided to confront these practices and to uproot them."

Mike awaited a reply from the international, and never received one.

—

Michael D.'s mother was not pleased. "No member of this family is going to live with a Nigger family," she told her son. She began crying, standing up from the kitchen table and pacing back and forth. She put a hand to her forehead and attempted speaking again. The words evaded her, and she went to the sink for a glass of water. When she turned back, she held her hands out before her. They were shaking. "Please! I'm pleading with you! Please don't do it!"

"But, Mom, I've never done anything like this. This is—"

"Nobody'll talk to me any more."

"Mom."

"All my friends. They'll ostracize me, all of them."

Michael D.'s mom had not been happy with his taking the class in the first place. "I demand that you change your schedule!" she said when she first heard about it. Michael D. refused, and then the truly unspeakable (for his mom) took place.

"My outward appearance isn't the typical conventional look. I have very long hair, drive an old van that still has faded lettering from an air conditioning business, and am also known to go shoeless at times. As a class, we've been conducting a survey of prejudice involved in procuring housing in Jacksonville. We sent mixed couples along with same-color couples, to look at rentals. The mixed and black couples have been turned away from most of the available rental properties. However, white couples (even me, the way I look!) have been accepted for the very same properties. None of us is surprised, but we *are* appalled nonetheless."

During this class assignment, Michael D. worked on occasion with Audrey, a young black woman also in the class. "I found her to be exciting, an attractive individual. I told my mother that I was planning to ask Audrey out. She was a lovely lady, and I knew it! But my mother pitched a fit. She actually pulled a gun on me. Just my entering the class had been too much for her, and now she threatened to kill me...and herself!...if I went out on a date with this girl."

Michael D. did not ask Audrey out. He had taken his mother's threat seriously. He does not tell us in his journal whether he ever explained the situation to Audrey herself. But he did think deeply in his writing about what this exchange demonstrated. "The roots of racism are so deeply entrenched in my family," he writes, and he later worries that those roots would disappear only when his parents died.

But then came the second crisis for Michael D. and his mother: the home visit.

Michael D. had been thinking for quite a while about Blacks and Whites and what they could learn from...and about...each other through the kind of direct contact that, so far in his life, only this class had provided. The difficult arguing in class with his fellow students, and then with his mother, the sudden revelations, the class cooling off periods spent in quiet, the students exhausted by the heat of the conversations...all of it had brought a flood of ideas and new feelings to him. It was tough. The class was very often a pressure cooker. His mother continued being very upset with him. But the class was giving him what he had been seeking, and he persisted despite the conflicts.

He wrote in his journal: "In the long run I knew the experience of living and associating with Blacks was the only way I could better understand them and their culture. All my white friends have the 'answers' for the Blacks. But I have come to the point of sheer boredom discussing the black and white situation with Whites because they either don't see the problem or have intellectualized answers for a people they know virtually nothing about."

Michael D. persisted, risking especially the wrath of his mother, because he felt so strongly about what he wished to learn from the home visit.

He found that he was to live with a black Baptist minister, Reverend Jordan, and his family. "I originally perceived the visit to be this: the white student goes into the ghetto, lives with a black family for six days, and comes out." Michael D. was willing enough. He wanted the experience. But his visit was to be far more than a cursory tour of a "ghetto," and he had little idea of the complexity of the things he would learn and, especially, the emotional effect those things would have on him.

"Dr. Kranz wants to force white students into contact with black families, on the family's terms, not on the student's. He's forcing people to confront each other as people...on the truly personal level. Minute by minute, you must relate to people as individuals, not as an abstract 'black family' or an abstract 'white middle class student.'"

Michael D. suffered a number of anxieties prior to the visit. He writes that he simply did not know what to expect. He worried how his "normal life pattern" was about to be upset. He knew very little about the family he was to visit, other than that the parents ran a nursery school. He was suffering the basic, and normal, fear of the unknown.

For one thing, the neighborhood he entered on his first day was not a "ghetto," as he had imagined it would be. It was indeed just a neighborhood, with small homes, many run-down, trees here and there, yards, space, sidewalks.

"I was welcomed warmly by the children in the neighborhood; actually, a scene of chaos as all the kids wanted to find out who I was and if they could help me. But the neighborhood *is* different from my own. Their lawns consist of sand, not manicured grass. The children were wearing well-worn clothes, maybe hand-me-downs. These are things I never experienced as a child. I was always expected to be spotlessly clean, and never was allowed to soil my clothes."

The first individual that Michael D. met as the home visit got under way was Reverend Jordan. A large, serious man wearing black slacks, a white dress shirt, a black tie, and black dress shoes, the minister stood in the front doorway to his home, taking up a large percentage of the space represented by the doorframe. He offered a thick hand to Michael D., who took it into his as he thanked the Reverend for accepting him into his home.

Michael D. had lived with a black person before, a young man with whom he had worked at a community center. They had gotten along quite well, so that Michael D. did not suffer from the sort of trepidation that other students in the class had, who had never been in a black or white home before. Michael D. realized, nonetheless, that the terms of this home visit were far more precise and direct than those of the previous experience with his friend at the community center. "This situation is different. I'm staying with a family precisely *because* of our racial difference. Because I'm *white*, not because I'm Michael D., I am staying for a week with the Jordans because they are *black,* not for any other reason. The very structure of the requirement makes our racial differences a barrier that has to be confronted. Our racial identities are *the* determining factor for our being paired up."

Clearly, Michael D. understood what was at stake. Given his own mother's deep anxieties about what this whole Human Conflict class thing was presenting to her son...and to her...he was well aware on an intimate family level of the racial situation in Jacksonville in that time. He wrote in his journal: "Whether or not race is a meaningful method of grouping people is a question very worthy of discussion. But it is a fact that people have been grouped [in this country] according to race, and our society is segregated according to race. So, I'm being forced to live for a week in direct contradiction to that segregation."

Reverend Jordan was seventy-three years old. "He does not appear or act like any seventy-three year old I've ever met." The house was reasonably large, old, and much lived in. Michael D. felt that the Jordans could have better furniture than the house contained, and he was soon to learn why they did not. It was a matter of allocating funds to things about which they cared far more deeply than couches and easy chairs.

The Jordans had two boys, both adopted. Michael D. became pals right away with Theodore, the younger son at ten years old. Theodore was a happy boy. Michael D. describes him as being "honest, open, and full of energy...very friendly." What Theodore wished for most was that he be paid attention to and his spirit and humor be acknowledged.

Michael, fourteen, was a more cautious child. Michael D. writes: "Apparently he has found that the honest, warm, outgoing presentation of yourself to others often results in being pushed away, or taken advantage of. It appears that, at some time in Michael's life, he learned that being black is just not something to be proud of."

When Reverend Jordan introduced the boys to Michael D., he mentioned that Michael was interested in sports...seriously interested. As Michael D. and Michael began talking with one another, Michael D. asked him which sports he preferred. He had loved Pop Warner football. He was now in his first year in junior high school, and told Michael D. he was planning to go out for the junior high school basketball team. Michael D. learned that, even more so than Reverend Jordan had indicated to him, Michael played sports with very serious intent. He got the impression that the boy felt his real value lay in sports and his ability to excel in them. This would be the forum in which Michael felt he could appear with distinction.

Later that day, Michael D. met Mrs. Jordan. A black woman in her mid-fifties, she was, as Michael D. was soon to learn, devoted to her husband and to the work they did together for the church community. She worked "harder than any twenty year-old I've ever seen," he writes. She rose early every morning to get her own two children ready for school, and then left the house precisely at 7:15 AM. The Jordans ran a nursery-kindergarten school that was part of Reverend Jordan's ministry, and Reverend Jordan himself would have left the house at 7:00, to prepare the school for the children...and to prepare breakfast for those children too poor to have received one at home. They owned a van that served as the church bus, and by 9:00 AM, Mrs. Jordan would have delivered the last of three vanloads of children to the school. Others would have been dropped off at school by their parents. Altogether, there were about one hundred children registered at the school, ages three months to six years, ninety percent of them black. The staff was made up of thirteen people: nine Blacks and four Whites.

Michael D. learned that Reverend Jordan's breakfast duties were no small matter. He prepared the morning meal every day for about eighty children, as well as some of their parents. Mrs. Jordan spent the majority of her day in the nursery, helping care for the youngest of the kids. At 3:30 PM, she would prepare the van for the first group of kids to go home. Then the second and the third. As a general rule, she arrived home herself at 7:30 PM every week day. "Twelve hours a day, five days a week," as Michael D. noted in his journal. Saturday was a bit better. The nursery-kindergarten was open for fewer hours on that day, so that Reverend and Mrs. Jordan were able to get home by 5:00. Sunday was the day of worship, of course. So the Jordans and their boys ministered to the churchgoers all day, every Sunday.

Mrs. Jordan explained the situation to Michael D. one evening as she was preparing dinner for the family. "'We run a nursery because there is a need for it,' she told me. 'The cost for the parents is lower than any other nursery in this area. It's the only one with bus service, at no extra charge. Parents pay more or less whatever they can.'"

All was not sanguine in the Jordan household. It was clear to Michael D. that the couple cared deeply for their own two sons. But fourteen year-old

Michael had been giving them problems for some years. One evening Reverend Jordan explained to Michael D. that their older son resented the fact of having been adopted. It was not so much the fault of his adoptive parents; rather he felt betrayed by the people who had brought him into the world. Why had he been abandoned? What did I do wrong to be left behind?

Reverend Jordan explained that he and his wife had made a fundamental error with the boy when he had been younger. "'We always bought him things, in compensation for his being so angry, for his acting out. But now we realize what we've done. It might be too late now, Michael D., because we still give in to his demands, and he still demands and hates'."

Hearing this, Michael D. was amazed...even somewhat sorrowful. Reverend and Mrs. Jordan, so selfless in their wish to help their community and its children, felt that they themselves were inadequate as parents, and that they had made the mistake of buying things for their boys, especially for Michael, in order to alleviate those faults. "They had gotten caught up in trying to buy love," he writes. Beyond this, Michael D. also felt the effects of a certain kind of privilege he had gained with the Jordans that he could not even have imagined just a few days before, when he had begun his home visit. "Their honesty in talking with me about these things was incredible."

An even bigger personal surprise was to come from Michael D.'s mother. On the Sunday afternoon of his home visit, he planned to take Theodore and Michael to the Jacksonville Zoo and Gardens. Michael D.'s brother James was twelve years old that year, and Michael D. invited him to come to the zoo also. He and the three boys spent a couple of hours wandering through the animal exhibits, and the boys celebrated each one by attempting imitations of the various animals' characteristics and voices.

Afterwards, Michael D. planned to take all three to his parents' home. He worried a great deal about how his mother would react, having two black boys in her house. He sensed that a moment could come in which his mother's anger would boil over, and she would insist that Theodore and Michael get out. A mere rejection would be bad enough. But Michael D. also worried that his mother could break out into language and actions that would be so insulting, so violent, that his own relationship with the boys could be put into jeopardy. But he also felt that there were large issues regarding race that his own family had to face. He sensed as well, having seen how Reverend and Mrs. Jordan had raised their boys in an atmosphere of true charitableness, that even despite Michael's emotional difficulties, the boys could withstand whatever Michael D.'s mom would possibly say.

But his mother brought the boys into the house and gave them ice cream sandwiches. Michael D. continued waiting for an outburst from her, which never came. She no longer seemed worried about what the neighbors would say. Indeed, one of them actually came over to the house, her own young boy in tow, whom she left playing with the others.

It sufficed for Michael D. merely to watch all this. He could not have imagined that his mother would react in so sanguine a manner. But she did, and he felt that somehow their arguments earlier about the class had caused her to open her mind to new possibilities. Ironically, he realized, this was one of the ultimate goals of the class itself for its students, with all its argument and confrontation.

At the end of the last day of his visit, Michael D. returned to his own home. He walked in the front door and dropped his knapsack to the floor. No one was there to greet him initially. But he heard his mother's voice, clearly involved in a telephone conversation. He walked up the hallway toward the kitchen and paused in the doorway.

His mother was making an arrangement with the person on the line, to get together sometime soon and, especially, to arrange for an outing together with the kids. Not wishing to interrupt, Michael D. waited. Finally his mother offered a warm good-bye to the person she was speaking with. "It's a pleasure for me too, Mrs. Jordan."

She hung up and turned around, surprised by Michael D.'s wide-eyed appearance in the doorway. Maybe a little embarrassed, happy to see him, she shrugged. "Well…I liked those boys," she said. "They gave me their mom's phone number."

A few weeks later, Michael D. returned to the Jordan nursery and began a series of art classes for the children.

—

Here following are some random observations by home hosts about the value of the home visit for them.

In 1972 Minor was a white professor at UNF, and he and his wife and three children were hosts to a young black student, Shelton. "I got from Shelton a window into what life was like when every single time you turn around, you are aware that people might be forming ideas about you based on the fact that you're a minority. I could understand in the abstract how that could be, but the persuasiveness of a very real view from the other side had never come home to me clearly. My discussions with Shelton were able to provide that."

Minor describes a kind of brief home visit of his own, the day that he drove to another student's house, a young man named Perry, to pick him up. "When I got there, I was invited into their house, and it was a very neat and clean place...but one that was also quite small. It showed signs of not having had very much money put into it. I could see the contrast that Perry was going to experience in just a few minutes when he arrived at our house, which by comparison was a much more affluent home. We were not rich by any stretch of the imagination, but certainly it was a more affluent home than Perry's family owned."

Minor points out that the neighborhood in which he and his family lived was *almost* exclusively white. A black UNF music professor lived in the neighborhood. "One of the reasons he could pull that off," Minor says, "was by virtue of his being with the university. Because of that, he was acceptable." With this description, one learns that the social class to which he/she belongs in certain instances can overcome the prejudice that results from ethnic difference. But at the time, the music professor's presence in that neighborhood was a rarity for Jacksonville.

At dinner one evening, Perry shared with Minor and his family his prior assumption, "that all white people were rich, and that he by comparison was poor. We had more space in our house, more affluence than in his. But Perry was struck by the fact that there was not quite the economic wealth in our place that he had expected."

Perry was also quite willing to offer opinions. "He did not just passively sit around. He sat down and engaged us in conversation about his visit, about the nature of it, about his reactions to it…and our reactions to him."

———

Rebecca was a thirty-two year-old black woman, divorced, with three children. She was host to a white student named Mary. "Here's how I viewed white people. I had grown up in an old black neighborhood and, of course, was black myself. I had not been around white people. I only saw them when they would come into the neighborhood for a specific purpose: like the bill collectors who came to my grandmother's house. That gave me a bad idea about what Whites were like."

Rebecca's children had a less problematic view of white people. "They were already involved in the changes that were taking place. They were being integrated [at school.] So they accepted the idea of this visit from a white person a lot better than I did, I believe. They got along well, more readily than myself. They had white school friends that would come over and visit them in our house, while other people in our neighborhood might not have allowed that. I knew several people, Blacks like us, that had reservations about this home visit idea. But the fact is, my children loved it!"

———

Pat was a divorced white woman with three teenaged sons. "My house was the best example of organized chaos that you ever saw. My boys were surfers, which in Florida was basically a white endeavor. When Phillip came to stay with us, we realized that he was not familiar with that world, and we learned that he was fascinated by it. I took him down to the beach to watch the boys surf, and he said 'This is really something!" I said, 'Yes, aren't they good?' and he shook his head and said, 'No, it's just that I've never seen a white mom involved with her kids the way you are.' I remember that remark more than anything. He was surprised that white people could do just like his mom or dad would."

Pat invited some white business associates to her home one evening.

They had learned of Pat's involvement with UNF and the idea of the home visit. (Phillip himself was not in attendance.) "I found out that they weren't as liberal as I had thought," she explained. "They were not accepting of the project, so really I had nothing to do with them socially again. Races just shouldn't mix, they said. I was shocked. They weren't at all the kind of people I had thought they were."

When Pat's oldest son got married some years later, Phillip was his best man. "He was very sweet," she recalls. "He always offered to help around the house, which one's own sons don't always do. But Phillip did."

—

Jack, the fifty-four year-old white man whom we met earlier in this chapter, describes his home visit. "They have to be very special people. It isn't easy to invite a total stranger to spend a full week living in your home with your family, someone you have never previously seen." After his visit, Jack had occasional phone conversations with acquaintances that were typical of the responses of many. "They knew I was taking the class, and there were a couple of people who wanted to know if I had really lived for a week with a 'Nigger' family. I finally had the opportunity to respond, 'Certainly. Why the hell not?' and then to proceed to point out to them that their racist opinions and ideas were groundless. It was propaganda that they had heard from others, things about which they actually knew nothing."

—

Ben, the Director of Admissions at UNF, and his wife and two children hosted four white students during the time of the class. Because of their association with the university and the fact that the Jacksonville public schools were being integrated through those years, Ben and his family had had significant contact with white people before any of the Human Conflict class members came into their home. The conversation around the dinner table, particularly when it came to racism, was spirited nonetheless, to say the least. "Racial things were discussed quite often," Ben recounts. "We were always doing that. Actual prejudices. The one thing that struck me was the racism that still exists. I knew that there was prejudice. I knew there was racism. But I did not understand how intense it still was, and the nonsensical nature of it. Believe me, those conversations made me realize it. Those students will share things with you. Even if you have your own ideas of what racism is about, we learned [from those discussions] that it is well beyond anything we still thought. For example, one of the white students staying with us explained how his parents had always told him never to get into a fight with a black person because all of them carried knives. And of course, you would always get that about black males. The sexual thing, too. We got deep into those kinds of racial things, and the surprise for me was how much the students thought that, for most of their fellow white people, those things would never change."

Ben asked for an example from one of the white students. "He told me this story: 'So it's 1972, and I'm white, and I have this black friend named Jerrod. He and I were discussing integration one evening, and I was telling him how much it had seemed to me that an integrated society was now the norm. I invited Jerrod to join me in a bar for a drink. It was then that he told me how he had gone to a bar in Jacksonville a few months before, in one of the white sections of town, and had gotten beaten up by the Whites there. So, when I invited Jerrod to join me that night, he wouldn't do it. He knew the intense racism that you could find in those places. He told me that white people couldn't change, regardless of what they did or said. They were all alike, he said.'"

—

One of the most painful home visits was one that actually never took place.

Martha, "that woman from Macclenny," dropped out of the class. Her leaving took everyone by surprise because she was perceived by most of the students as having made significant progress in her attitudes toward Blacks, her own white upbringing, and most particularly herself. Rex, the black student in the class who early addressed Martha as "that woman from Macclenny," had by now formed a different opinion of her. "On our first day [in class]," he writes, "she was very reclusive, even being reluctant to come to the aid of another white person." Her uncertainty about her personal value continued, in Rex's opinion, as he wrote at the time in his journal. "Martha isn't as mature as many. She is slower in her understandings, but she is striding and growing."

And then, she left.

Rex was particularly upset by this, and says so in his journal. The person he blames is Pete Kranz.

For some reason that she does not divulge to her own journal, Martha's home visit experience was the source of her leaving. We don't know what happened, although the conjecture of some in the class is that her parents' attitudes toward black people caused her to be unable to stay in a black home. They had forbidden her to do so, they surmise.

Rex feels that Pete did not do enough to help Martha through this crisis. "I'm highly impressed by Dr. Kranz in many ways. He is really someone I would like to have as a friend, mainly because he is someone who will not placate you simply because of your feelings. I admire his candor and direct personality…but…."

Rex's journal entry here becomes a series of individual sentences, with open spaces in between, as though he is writing, and then thinking about what he has said, and writing more, all the while affixing blame. What becomes evident is the development he has made in his feelings for Martha, his respect for her, and his wish that her self-confidence be protected and bolstered. "In my eyes, and I'm often wrong, Dr. Kranz is a cop-out artist. Regardless of his conversations with Martha of Macclenny, he should have tried to persuade her to stay in class." Rex pauses a moment. There is a space between one line in his journal and the next. And he then continues. "He never should have given up a member of the family, just due to her immature uncertainty." He pauses again…another space. "She knew she would fail without the home visit."

Rex then follows with an assessment of the situation that is unusual among the students in its fault-finding with Pete, but resounding in the candor with which Rex is able to put his feelings down on paper, especially in view of the fact that he knows Pete will be reviewing his journal. "I look at this class as Pete's pet project. But one factor goes bad, and he gives it up. If Martha were his daughter, he wouldn't have given up so easily. I know he will have a defense for his cop-out, and will say that he was simply respecting her decision."

This is actually so. Pete always stated clearly that a student could leave the class at any time for any reason. Nonetheless, Rex wishes that, in this case, Pete had attempted to keep her. "He just accepted her leaving without really trying to rebuild her confidence." Again, there is an open space in Rex's writing, a pause in it. "It was apparent in class. When they found out [that Martha had left], they resented the loss of a family member. We all want our family member back."

THE HISTORICALLY BLACK COLLEGE VISIT
"For the first time, I could hear what Blacks were saying."
—a white male student.

For white people in the United States, the initials "HBCU" may not be readily understandable. It is safe to say, however, that all black Americans who care about education know exactly what an HBCU is. The Higher Education Act of 1965 defines it as "any historically black college or university that was established prior to 1964, whose principal mission was, and is, the education of black Americans, and that is accredited by a nationally recognized accrediting agency or association determined by the Secretary [of Education] to be a reliable authority as to the quality of training offered or is, according to such an agency or association, making reasonable progress toward accreditation." The legalese that runs through this description does little to hide the true educational purpose of an HBCU and the singular importance these institutions have had, and continue to have, for advanced education in the United States.

There are approximately one hundred such institutions in the U.S., almost all of them located in the South. They came about from necessity. After 1877, education for Blacks was largely neglected by the white citizenry and the representative governments of the southern states. Blacks, after all, had been legislated into a position in which they had little, if any, representation. They simply could not get into white schools. So Blacks took it upon themselves to provide education to their children.

A kind of educational self-help system, in which Blacks taught Blacks on an ad. hoc. basis, was to suffice for a while. An actual public education system for Blacks in the South had been established by the federal government even as the Civil War was in its last throes. In March 1865, two years after the Emancipation Proclamation was signed by Abraham Lincoln, the Freedmen's Bureau was established by Congress with the purpose of directing "such issues of provisions, clothing, and fuel, as [may be deemed] needful for the immediate and temporary shelter and supply of destitute and suffering refugees and freedmen and their wives and children." One of the very important mandates of this organization was to found and maintain public schools for the children of those who had previously been slaves.

By 1870, the Freedmen's Bureau had established more than one thousand such schools in the South. Funds were forthcoming from the federal government, although they were insufficient for the scope of what the Bureau wished to achieve. Even as their financial situation was so often dire, Blacks came together to donate funds, find land, and build schools on their own.

But with the end of Reconstruction in 1877, the federal attention to the need for quality education waned. Nonetheless, private funds from individual Whites and white-owned organizations were eventually forthcoming. One of the largest eventual such programs was the Julius Ronsenwald Fund, which was established in 1914. Rosenwald was one of the earliest principal owners and eventual president and chairman of the board of Sears Roebuck and Company. He was a friend of Booker T. Washington, the principal founder of Tuskegee Institute in Alabama, and was named by Washington to the institute's board of directors, a position he held for the rest of his life. Further urged by Washington to become involved in efforts to provide proper education to black children in the South, Rosenwald began by offering funds to build six primary schools for black children in rural Alabama. His interest was more than philanthropic; it was deeply personal. He had written, "The horrors that are due to race prejudice come home to the Jew more forcefully than to others of the white race, on account of the centuries of persecution which they have suffered and still suffer." The school building program became one of the largest administered by the Rosenwald Fund. It contributed in excess of four million dollars in matching funds (offered by other individuals and organizations) to the construction of more than five thousand schools, shops, and teachers' homes in the South.

Providing higher education for their children was an equally important goal to black people. Since white colleges and universities more or less excluded Blacks, Blacks themselves founded those institutions that eventually fell under the rubric of "HBCU." These schools were not exclusively the result of the Civil War. Indeed Cheney University and Lincoln University were founded in Pennsylvania in 1837 and 1854 respectively, while Wilberforce University was founded in Ohio in 1856. The very first HBCU to be established in the South was Shaw University in Raleigh, North Carolina, founded in 1865. Although a significant percentage of funds for the founding of these schools often came from white individuals, white-run charities and religious organizations, and white-owned businesses, the principals involved in founding them and running them were for the most part black, as were the student bodies.

No HBCU excludes anyone from attending for reasons of race.

—

Pete Kranz required a visit for each of his classes to an HBCU. The first such took place at Albany State College in Albany, Georgia. The purpose of the HBCU visit was two-fold. One was to bring the black students in the class into an institute of higher learning in which Blacks formed the great majority of the faculty and student body, thus making them the ascendant group, racially, in the institution. They were in the majority and in control. The second purpose was to allow white students to understand the educational integrity of these schools and to have the experience of being a distinct minority.

The students were driven to Albany state in a mini-bus. Pete Kranz was at the wheel, and during the trip there was a good deal of singing, story-telling, laughter, napping…. One student recalls the journey: "I remember enjoying watching people's faces as our 'zebra' family drove by. What did those conservative Whites think we were all about? And what about the Blacks, did they think some sort of cultural uprising was taking place? We were lucky not to have been harassed by rednecks in passing cars or while we were making a pit stop."

As one of the students, a white female named Danielle, writes in her journal, "It is a strange experience to be the only white face in an all-black environment. I say 'strange' because what occurred very quickly was that I forgot I was white. I forgot I didn't look like all those around who were hurrying to get to class. So I was surprised therefore to be looked at oddly, the unspoken words nonetheless written on the black students' faces, 'What is that honky doing here?'"

The students would be staying in dorms at Albany State, and four of them on this particular trip were women: two Blacks and two Whites. Danielle had been raised in a household in which personal modesty was insisted upon, and she would be sharing one of the dorm rooms with a black woman classmate. Even this was a moment of "racial confrontation" of a sort because she had never been less than fully clothed in the company of black people. "I felt the need to explain to her that my insecurity had nothing to do with color. 'Even as a kid,' I said, 'I used to dress and undress under the covers.'"

"What about when you were at someone's house, though, you know, going for a swim or something," her roommate asked, smiling.

"Then, I'd change in a closet."

Her roommate laughed, and explained that she had been brought up in a similar way.

On Friday at noon of their visit to Albany State, the students gathered to go to lunch. They had been invited to the cafeteria, and this would be their first exposure to the Albany State students, and their first appearance, Whites and Blacks together, in a public room at the school. Surprise and silence on the part of the Albany State students were the reactions at first. The surprise was immediate. The silence lasted for a while. "We were stared at and no doubt gossiped about right away," one student recalls. The UNF students proceeded to the cafeteria line for lunch, and a combination of laughter, curiosity, and, it seemed especially to the white students, suspicion followed them. They attempted remaining cool and sophisticated-seeming. Their arrival in the cafeteria was clearly unexpected by the majority of the Albany State students. "Yes, we were gossiped about," another student writes. "But eventually we were just ignored, and everybody went on with their lunch."

As they were proceeding with their trays to an open table, the students were startled when one young Albany State man jumped up onto the table where he had been seated, and began beating on a garbage can lid. "He was ranting," one of the white students remembers. "I hunkered down right there with the other white girl, and we averted our eyes." The two worried that they and the other Whites had "invaded the space" of the Albany State students, and that maybe a riot was in progress because of that. The young black man continued shouting and beating rhythmically on the garbage can lid. Others joined him, stamping their feet, and the two girls worried that a violent political demonstration might be underway, and that they and the others from UNF—especially the Whites—were the cause of it. The shouting continued. "It was unnerving and loud."

Mike, one of the white students, describes the moment in his journal. "The experience was something about which the black and white students together felt humiliated at first. We thought people were pounding on the tables because white people were in the room. I personally felt awkward, and I think the black UNF students felt humiliated because it was their own people behaving this way. I just kept thinking, boy! there's got to be a better way of putting people together."

Ann writes in her journal about this event a few days later. "I have mixed feelings. The disgraceful cheers that rang through the cafeteria did not impress me as being those of an oppressed people, but instead of people who are hung up on letting others know who the boss is here. I say, 'The boss of what?'"

Quickly, the two white women began making out the words of the shouting and screaming. "Beat Fort Valley! Beat Fort Valley!" One pointed to a large paper banner that covered much of the wall at one end of the cafeteria. "Albany State Golden Rams! Homecoming!" were the words on the banner, painted in watercolors blue and gold. The students continued chanting and shouting, and the sense of jubilation and excitement that the homecoming was providing for them suddenly became obvious to the UNF students. The violent political demonstration was indeed a raucous, spirit-building celebration of the football game that was to be contested later that afternoon.

The UNF students were invited to the game. It happens that Albany State beat Fort Valley that day 30-14. The game was a riotous outburst of fun for every Albany State fan present, including those from UNF.

After the game, the UNF students were urged to go into Albany's central shopping district together, in a group, to look around. Harold, a black middle class student whose parents both had college degrees, was in the company of one of the white women students. He later recalled, "As I remember, she was a little older than I at the time…mid-twenties. I knew, because of our time in class, that she had a fear of black men, deep-down fear. One day in class she broke down in tears as she admitted her fears to us. So, in downtown Albany, we were walking around together, and she saw how those white folks were looking at her so hard. She grabbed my hand, out of fear. But it was not for fear of black folks; this time it was fear of white folks."

"I don't know," she said when Harold asked whether she felt all right. "Fear is fear, Harold. No matter who the perpetrator is, it's still fear."

Harold continued holding her hand. "This was good," he recalls. "Very good. Being able to express yourself the way she did, and both of us able to learn from it."

Harold describes as well the reaction he and his fellow student got from many black people at the football game. "My family went to black colleges, and it was part of the lifestyle [that they provided for me]. Being teamed up with a white female, I was reminded of how prejudiced black people could be…and a lot of white people in this world don't know about that. I used to sit in class listening to the back and forth, and think, if all the white people who hired black folks to cook for them knew how much they were hated, they'd never hire anybody black to do that. So, at the football game, I got some looks from black girls that, if those looks could kill, I'd be gone! But even that was a positive of a kind. They did not understand what we were doing together that day, and by their not understanding, we got their very true, up-front feelings."

Philip, a black student, tells of one other moment of revelation that occurred during the football game. "It was stressful. We saw the white students sticking a little closer to us, because at that point, they became the center of attention. They were uncomfortable, yet we Blacks were comfortable there, and they were depending on us."

—

One personal event during the trip to Albany was a real positive for Ann. "It was after I had returned home that I realized that, for the first time in my life, I had shared a room with a white person. Now I ask myself, 'What in hell was the difference?' The answer? There was none."

-7-

THE TRUTH, CONSIDERED

"I think we are going backwards today on racial issues, rather than forward. In the 1970s, what you saw was in essence what you got. I think people now tend to be more covert with their feelings. They put on a false front. They are not as genuine."

—a former black student

"That class? It was an arena of truth."

—a former black student

W hat did all this mean to the students years later?
Pete Kranz conducted a series of interviews in 1993 with nineteen of his former UNF students: ten Whites and nine Blacks. Most were in mid-career. The purpose was to determine from them what lasting impressions they still had of the class. What had it done for them and their understanding of the racial issues that caused them to come to the class in the first place? Where had it not had an effect? What did they have to say about it now?

In 2017, I too interviewed several former students. By now, for the most part, these people are retired, well into middle age or older. I asked them a single question: How did this class affect the rest of your life?

—

Marguerite describes some very important events in her life after Pete Kranz's class.

"The day I walked into the class, in 1973, I think I had a kind of awkward politeness around white people, in which no matter what Whites may have done in the past, you still maintained that awkward politeness. But that was a barrier that I was able to shed because of the class.

"In 1976, I moved to Tallahassee, Florida, to work for the state government. There was an incident one day, in which a white supervisor treated one of her black employees in a way that I didn't feel was fair. At first I didn't think I should get involved. You know, stay out of it, Marguerite. It's not your business.

"But then, a while later, I myself was up for a promotion. At the time, I had two years of college education. I was to be interviewed by my white supervisor, who was a woman I knew, a woman I worked with every day. When the interview started, she asked me one or two questions, and then her phone rang. She picked up the receiver, and it was clear to me that this was a personal call, from a friend or someone. I waited, and continued waiting, until the scheduled time for the interview to close arrived. She was still on the phone. She interrupted the conversation, to end the interview. That was it! I was out of there!

"Another woman in our section was also interviewed, someone who started with the state just a few days after I started. She had a high school diploma. She was white, and she got a full interview...no phone call. And she got the job.

"I went right to the Equal Employment Opportunity Commission."

This federal organization had been founded during the presidency of Lyndon B. Johnson. Part of its mandate, under Title VII of the Civil Rights Act of 1964, was to administer and enforce civil rights laws against workplace discrimination.

"I may not have done that, had it not been for Pete's class," Marguerite says. "It was a confidence I now had, about not feeling that awkwardness I talked about, when it came to dealing with this particular white supervisor. Maybe she thought I should have been grateful for simply having gotten the interview. But I felt that the supervisor and I were on the same playing field, and I won the case! The EEOC said I should have gotten the job. I got the back pay, and everything that went along with it.

"Now this was supposed to be a supervisory position, and when I finally got there, I learned that there was no supervision involved, and that basically nothing for me had really changed. So I complained again. This time, the position was restored to what it was supposed to be, and an EEOC officer was also to become part of our department staff.

"This was great. But then there was a new statewide election, and the new Secretary of State declared that he was under no obligation to honor any agreement made by his predecessor.

"So I sued the State, for discrimination against black Americans in hiring and promotion. I got eighteen people, all black and all representative of the areas of employment in that part of the government, and we did a class action suit. (By the way, except for two of those people, who were senior aids to government officers, the rest of us worked in the basement of the old state building—a new one had just been built—and we were kept unseen.) The class action lasted for nineteen years, and at the end of that, those whose names were still connected with it received a suitable settlement. It happens that I myself had left the suit. Our attorney explained to me that, because I had gotten some compensation from my first suit, the possibility for my getting additional compensation could hamper the progress of this class action suit. So I dropped out. I didn't want to get in the way.

"In the meantime, a lot because of the class action, conditions changed in the State government's hiring and promotions practices.

"I never felt isolated after that. I didn't have that awkwardness. And I think a lot of what I did in those times was due to 'Human Conflict: Black and White.'"

—

In 1993, Pete interviewed Jim, the one-time liberal who was involved in the lettuce boycotts of the early 1970s. By the time of the interview, he had spent a dozen years as a policeman on the Jacksonville force, and was now a small retail-business owner. "I remember as a police officer, the older black people would still call me 'sir.' The younger ones, my own age, weren't as militant as they had been in the 1960s and 70s. No, during those years, they would spit at you."

Jim thinks that the family values that he learned about during the class, especially during the home visit, had disintegrated by 1993. He thinks that, among young Blacks in that year, "they have no sense of value at all. No family. It's a single-parent situation most of the time, and the kids are unsupervised. I think we're in a crisis in Jacksonville, and that division between the races is becoming much more prevalent again."

—

Rebecca, a black woman who hosted a white woman, Mary, later explained in an interview how the experience of being a host actually changed her attitude about whether or not she could mix with Whites. She was an assistant teacher at the time. "Mary and I shared our feelings and our past history. I told her that I was brought up by my grandmother, and I had taken on some of her values about being a hard worker, in order to keep the family from being on welfare. It meant a lot to me not to have to accept help from others." Rebecca had never spoken with a white person about this. "We shared our feelings," she said in the interview. "And it brought us closer together."

The times were changing. By the mid-1970s, schools were being integrated in Jacksonville, and Rebecca's young children were now pupils in integrated schools. "They accepted my white house-guests better than I did, I think. Mary's visit made it even easier for them to accept Whites than it already was for my kids. There were several people that I knew…Blacks like us…that had reservations about this home host thing. But Mary and I, we talked mostly personal. It was a wonderful experience for me."

Rebecca's life changed when her son David eventually married a white woman, and at the time of the interview, she had one granddaughter from that marriage. "I love my granddaughter's mother, and I truly believe that after being part of Pete's class, I was very prepared to accept this. I think that, had I not participated in the class, I would have had reservations about what my son was doing. But I don't."

Rebecca also describes a practice in her own teaching that she got from the class. "I run an extended day-care now, before and after school, and I bring in Whites and Blacks at the same time, in order to let them be aware of each other. It's because of that home visit. I believe everyone at all ages should open up their hearts and their homes to each other, to see what the other group's lives are all about. It would become a much better world."

—

Ann, whom we first met on her first day as a student in the first 1972 class, later became a home host for white students from subsequent classes. In an interview in 1996, she expressed a unique view of something she had observed in her hosting of students. "In the black community [with regard to Whites] we functioned on what had actually happened to us, in real life. A lot of the Whites were functioning on beliefs [about Blacks] that were based on conditions about which they basically knew nothing." She reveals that the class was nonetheless of great value because of what it taught her about Whites…and about herself. "Situations that are that intense, you don't realize the true impact of it while it is happening. But I know that, for me and others, that impact actually lasted for much longer than just the life of the class itself."

She talks also about an ironic series of interactions she made while hosting white students in her home, of which over the years there were several. "My children had no problem because they were in integrated day-care facilities, and my youngest son, whom I adopted, was a bi-racial kid. So that made it a lot different. It did have an impact on the neighborhood kids. They wanted to know why all these white people were staying in our home. The complexions of my family range from very dark to very light, so I introduced some of our home visit guests as my relatives, or my husband's relatives."

Perhaps the most important element in the home visit experience, if not the entire class, was the dispelling of prejudices that, without these experiences, might well have gone unaddressed. The reputation of the town of Macclenny as a center for blatant white racism against Blacks came up once again for another white Macclenny resident who participated in the class, because of the way he spoke. "My children liked Ricky," Ann says, "*because* he had such a southern drawl."

It may not have seemed at first that Ricky would be welcomed in the neighborhood. He writes in his journal, "The first thing I noticed was a group of neighbors watching me get out of the car. I had the feeling the whole neighborhood was watching me." When he entered the Hursts' home, he was greeted by Ann and Rodney's son, Rodney Jr. (then five years old) who asked, "Is it true that you are afraid of black women?"

"Usually I'm quick-witted enough to think of *something* to say," Ricky writes. "But this child got the best of me right off."

"He was really a nice person," Ann recalls. "But you wouldn't know it at first, just listening to him. The kids liked him because the accent was so funny. At first they thought they were really going to have a problem with him, with that drawl. But no, not at all." At first, Ann and her husband Rodney worried about Ricky and what sort of person he was. "We expected to have the biggest problems with him, because of the way he spoke. But, you know, he was the most open one of all."

Ricky confides to his journal a wish he has that, for his Macclenny acquaintances, must remain secret, at least for the moment. "I've decided to take the blonde I've been dating over to meet Ann and Rodney and their kids. But we won't mention it to her daddy. At least not until he gets to know me better." One can wonder what the visit might have been like had Ricky invited his girl friend's father along as well.

Unexpected relationships were not uncommon as a result of the home visit. Ann describes one of the white female students who stayed with her and her family. "She wouldn't let go of that uncomfortableness. We tried, but…. Then a white girlfriend of hers came to visit, which I think gave us a kind of protection. And that girl is now one of my family's closest friends. She came, and we got to know her. She's a missionary now…a dear friend."

—

Philip used the experience of the class as an opportunity to demonstrate to himself something that he had little considered before, about himself and, he hoped, all black people. He describes an internal conflict with which he was dealing at the time. "Often as a black person, you say to yourself, 'Well, I want to get away from certain things.' And so we start looking at elements in our own life as being bad...something we want to get away from. And the class helped me to deal with some of my own prejudices against my own race."

Those prejudices had been part of his thinking before the Albany State visit. But after the visit, Phillip began reconsidering them. "I had thought that black schools were all party types of things, and that people weren't learning anything there. I just allowed myself to be polluted by all that. But you know, in a way [the result] was good for me in the end, because now I understood that I was missing some of the things that I could have had at an all-black college. But on the other hand, I also thought that, having been taken out of our black world and put into a white—well...integrated— world, this was a chance to let these white people see what black people are all about. That was helpful, because I wanted them to come onto my ground, and to see the difference."

Phillip also describes a source of discomfort for him, which the class allowed him to explore and resolve. "What was uncomfortable was having to deal with the way *you* felt, and not about how people felt about you. How did *you* feel about this or that type of person? And how could *you* verbalize that in a mixed group? Prior to that, you were probably coming from an environment in which you were told that you just should *not* say certain things about certain people...especially *to* those people. All of a sudden, I'm being encouraged to say how I really feel. That was the most threatening thing to me. But it worked."

—

Clifford describes the effect on him of some of the more pointed conversations in which he was involved. "When we sat on the floor in a circle, some of those conversations were tough experiences because they had pointed questions, things for which you really had to do some introspection. You had to really dig to find just where you stood. You thought sometimes that you knew where you stood, but when you looked at all the sides, you thought 'My goodness, maybe I don't believe this after all!' This is when you need to get off dead center, and it forces you into making a decision. So in retrospect, these sessions gave me the guts to meet some of the challenges, and to accept some of the challenges, that I am faced with even now."

One of those challenges for Clifford lies in what he sees among the present generation of black youths. "I was speaking to a group of young kids the other day. They wanted to know about how different it is now from when I was their age. I said that the changes are good…and bad. Good from the perspective that they have the opportunity now to get jobs and earn money that they would not have had back then. They can live where they want. But that's not what Dr. King died for, and I see those opportunities as also being abused. We are becoming a lot more independent from our roots…forgetting them. We're being absorbed into the dominant culture to the point that there is little difference between us and the others. That's all right as long as the playing field is level for all of us. But looking at it just from the monetary aspect and what the system can do for you, you disregard where others are, as well as trying to help them excel. You get bought out by the money."

Clifford pauses a moment. Silence pervades his breathing as he thinks about what next to say.

"That's why we need those classes again."

—

Cary, the white student who said on the first day of class, "Blacks piss me off. I feel they expect and demand a free ride" was interviewed in1993. "In high school, I lived in Ocean Way, out toward the airport. It was still rural out there, and I can remember having KKK rallies right close to our neighborhood. The uncle or father of one of the neighborhood kids was a Grand Dragon. There were no Blacks in my junior high school, and only one or two in my high school graduating class. My perceptions were that

I was not a racist. I wasn't a bigot. Because, you know, I felt I just wasn't that kind of person."

Cary recalled how, as a child during several summers, he had visited an uncle who was a farmer in Georgia. Cary had a friend there, a young black boy his own age who was the son of one of his uncle's hands. "It was very paternalistic. All my clothes that I outgrew, we always took them up to Georgia, and my uncle would distribute them to his black farmhands. Clothes. Toys. My friend was Russell. We would play in the barn and ride mules. But of course when it came time for dinner, he went home, and I remember asking why couldn't he eat with us? And I'd see him at the movies on Saturday, and he'd have to sit upstairs, while I had to sit downstairs. He was my only friend, but I had to sit through the movies by myself, because I was down here, and he was up there.

"So I grew up thinking I didn't have anything against black people. That's just what I thought. But now I know that wasn't true. And it was the class that changed me."

What specifically changed Cary was the confrontational nature of the conversation. "The group discussions, especially when I had to share something of myself. I wasn't real fond of that." Pete and the other students wouldn't let Cary remain silent or inexpressive. "Peer pressure. You had to explore these feelings on some kind of level, and you couldn't come across real phony about it because I remember Pete would call us out on that kind of stuff. It was scary. And the uncomfortable part was when I had to face up to my belief that, even though I grew up in the South, I was not a bigot or a racist. That I was not brought up with any particularly negative perception of Blacks. And what I found out in the class was that I did have such perceptions! There was a continual battle between how I was raised and what I was learning."

One of the most telling developments in Cary's experience was the friendship he developed with Carlton, one of the very militant black students in the Human Conflict class. "The odd thing was that we liked each other. He had lived in Southeast Asia...been in business there...played in a band there. He was a military veteran. He had traveled. An interesting guy. The way I viewed Blacks? And the way I perceived the stereotypes? Well,

I can pinpoint that class as definitely changing my opinions…along with Carlton's influence on my attitudes."

—

In an interview, one black woman former student describes her view of what Blacks and women can expect to find now when entering the corporate world. Ultimately she views the difficulties that still exist as justification for instituting the kinds of racial confrontation—or gender confrontation—sessions as those that were developed for the Human Conflict class. "Divide and conquer. I think corporate America uses that today. Sure, there are black CEOs now. But if you want to keep a Black down there, or a woman, then keep them there. At least back then, in the 1970s, you had Blacks and a lot of empathetic Whites walking the same line. But women had their own cause to fight, which separated them [from the corporate world] the way all Blacks had been previously. It is still divide and conquer. America is still ruled by white men over forty. If that situation is jeopardized in any way, they change the game. And that's why we need these kinds of confrontation groups today…everywhere, at all levels."

—

There are very occasional observations about the class that indicate that the issues being discussed went right over the heads of a few students. One white female student shared the following during an interview some years later: "I enjoyed the class very much. It was a very interesting experience, especially the openness of the interplay of the people. Some things that I had always thought about prejudice—but had never heard voiced between Blacks and Whites—came out." This woman then does not respond, with any specific observations, to questions aimed at illustrating what indeed she had learned during these class sessions. Almost everything she says is complementary, distant, well mannered, bland, and without conviction.

—

Harold, one of the black students from the very first class, went on to a seventeen-year career in law enforcement, after which he became a teacher. In an interview, he explained a few things he once felt about white people and himself. "White people, you had to deal with them in order to survive, no matter how much you feared or disliked them. So I had to know my enemy, and that was white folks. I had to know them better than they know themselves, in order to travel in their world. Before I took the class, I was unable to put together an effective conversation with a white person. This class gave me insight as to who they were, how they were, and what they had the capabilities of being."

Considering that this possibly meant that, before taking the class, Harold really did *not* know the enemy well, gave him an insight to why the class was in the end so valuable to him.

"I learned there that I could talk about anything, because it was obvious to me that our brain capacity, our intelligence…I mean for both races…is not based on the color of our skin. Your color has nothing to do with these things, and I learned that there. It set the tone for how I was going to deal with whomever, no matter their race. It sounds dramatic, but that's what the course did for me."

—

"You know, those past feelings I had," one black student explains some years later, "of defensiveness, holding judgmental opinions, and generalizations based on color, were just simply replaced in my mind by more accurate considerations based on a person's individual qualities." This man went on to become a manager in a government agency, and he explains how what he learned in class affected his entire career in working with people who worked for him. "Many types of people. Now, I no longer blame a whole race of people because of the actions of a few. Prejudices are still active today. The class helped me to identify those prejudices when they appear and to face them. I was less afraid to exert myself publically. I felt comfortable confronting others and holding them to the real issues. And color has been negated as an element in my decisions."

—

A white corporate manager who had been in the class spoke about his own racism, which, he freely offered, had been an active element in his thinking as a younger man. "Occasionally, I'm still treated prejudicially by minorities. Some individuals still think that all Whites are 'anti-minority,' and being treated this way still angers me. But I'm more tolerant of it now than I would have been had I not experienced the activities, the interactions in that class."

—

One former student describes a personal crisis that the class presented to him, for which he remained grateful years later. "During those class sessions, I had to look deep inside myself and listen to my own words. I could stay where I was, or move on into uncharted territory. Scary, yes. But I moved to another level and shifted my focus from the external to the internal. That class made me take personal responsibility, and I can still hear things coming from my classmates so many years ago. Class members came alive...individually!...rather than remaining generalized in the eyes of others by the color of their skin."

—

The black student Rex went on to law school and a career as a practicing attorney, and talks about how the class prepared him for what was to come to him professionally. "It got me ready for the way business is done today. It prepared me for law school and the legal profession. It actually gave me a leg up on my professional contemporaries."

—

One student summed up the opinions of almost all those who were interviewed, of both races: "The class empowered us to challenge social injustices, to become change agents, and take more personal—and public—responsibility." Asked about what he would change in the class, he replies "Why would anyone want to change what has proven to be so successful? This was the mid-seventies. The idea of sharing living quarters with a black family in the deep South? It was very edgy, for them and for me. *Very* edgy. I run into former classmates now and then, and invariably we discuss what happened there. The class—if we did it properly...and most of us did—defines who we are."

—

In the case of almost all the students interviewed, memories of the class were clear and the analysis of it precise. Here following is a general summation of responses.

Many former students expressed the notion that specific racial or ethnic situations were proven *not* to be an ultimate hindrance to basic human relations. White and black students alike believed, to their surprise, that they found more similarities among each other than differences. To get to this understanding, though, direct confrontation was the key.

Before taking the class, white students particularly had voiced specific anxieties and fears about their black counterparts. But especially with the home visits, those fears were found to be without merit. The home visit and the visit to a black college indeed provided opportunities for positive personal change in the white students' ideas about racial difference. But the class discussions had a profound effect as well. One student said, "In class, I was surprised that the beliefs I had were so openly questioned. Many of those beliefs were not at all founded on reality. They were simply attitudes I had."

Students of both races stated that, prior to the beginning of the class, they felt real anxiety about freely stating their positions on race. None of them had ever done this in the presence of someone of the other race. The surprise came when, despite the arguments, the back-and-forth hostility, and often difficult interaction that could result, the students came away *not* feeling chastised for what they had expressed; rather, once a common demand for inclusion in each other's existence became a given, differences of opinion were more readily accepted. "Yes, we fought," one of the students said. "But it was ultimately for positive change."

Meaningful relationships between students grew stronger across ethnic lines. This happened most particularly after the visits to all-black colleges. Blacks were pleased to demonstrate the quality of those institutions, and to have that quality acknowledged and admired by their white cohorts. Whites were finally able to understand, and to contemplate at length, what it feels like to be an ethnic minority.

Although often noisy and argumentative, the class gave the students the opportunity to speak with each other frequently, openly, and directly about complex racial issues. This allowed for cohesiveness in working together on what were admittedly sensitive personal matters. "Over time, we were able to let our guard down," one former student says. "What had previously been quite conscious barriers to any meaningful communication disappeared. Not always; but usually." Almost all the students feel that, by the end of the class, they were much better prepared to step out into the wider world.

Confrontation was the key.

−8−

THE CURRENT MOMENT

"Although most of [these policies] are now off the books, they have never been remedied and their effects endure."
—Richard Rothstein, from *The Color of Law: A Forgotten History of How Our Government Segregated America,* 2017

"Looking inside wasn't easy, but it was a real awakening. This awakening has lasted a lifetime."
—a white student.

The classes continued at UNF for six years and, although a few students did drop out along the way, the great majority of them stayed for the whole semester, and applauded what the class had done for them. Almost to a person, those interviewed years later say that it is the one class they remember in detail. What they cherish most is that they were able to discuss with each other directly all the racial issues that had separated previous whole generations from each other. Those issues were difficult, and were addressed in the class with straightforward and often flinty intensity. None of the students had ever even considered the possibility of such conversations prior to taking the class.

The method worked.

Indeed, the classes constitute a kind of revolution in thinking for these one hundred-plus participants, in the sense that they brought about changes in the thought and actions of those involved that had seldom been seen, if ever, among Americans previously. However, as Coretta Scott King observed, "Struggle is a never-ending process. Freedom is never really won; you earn it and win it in every generation." A gracefully stated truth, in the context of "Human Conflict: Black and White," it leads to the obvious question: "What about now?"

—

I am writing this on September 5, 2017, three and a half weeks after the horrific events in Charlottesville, Virginia and just a few minutes after learning that the president of the United States has declared DACA (Deferred Action for Childhood Arrivals) a dead letter. A federal program that benefits 800,000 self-registered children of immigrants that entered the United States illegally for whatever reason, DACA has been given six months to live. Deportation of those thousands is a distinct possibility. This comes in almost the same presidential moment as when, then a candidate, the same man declared that a wall would be built along the entirety of the Mexico-United States border. This would be done in order to keep Mexicans and other brown people at bay on their side of the line, people who would like to fill jobs in the United States that American citizens themselves disdain and moreover are untrained for, due to their basic lack of interest and of a recognizable work ethic. Contractors have been approached by the government, to submit proposals for building the wall.

Also the president is trying to get laws passed that would severely alter immigration policies and practices that have been in place for decades, the results of which have brought millions of highly trained and/or motivated immigrants into this country. Those being acted against by this particular presidential whim are almost universally Muslim.

A more homespun endeavor by some, to reduce the voting strength of the political party now out of power and of certain minority groups—particularly Blacks—is currently finding purchase in many states. It is a new take—sophisticated and technology-driven—on an old practice.

In 1812, Elbridge Gerry, a white man, was the governor of the state of

Massachusetts. A wealthy landowner, he was one of the signatories of the Declaration of Independence. As governor, he wished to rearrange the voting districts in Massachusetts in order to insure that his own political party would be able to maintain its influence throughout the state in future elections. An inventive re-drawing of the state's voting district maps brought this about, although these new maps had little relationship to actual geographical realities like rivers, streams, mountains, and ocean shores. Rather, Gerry's maps would arrange voting districts in such a way that his party's own constituency could maintain a majority, or at least a very strong influence, in almost every newly designed district, no matter the actual lay of the land. What Gerry may not have thought about was the possibility that an opposing party could, through some fluke, win a future election, thus allowing it to restructure districts in its own way, differently. But so it has gone, into the present time.

The practice was given the name "to gerrymander," thus immortalizing Elbridge Gerry's name. The second part of the term comes from the amphibian lizard "salamander" and its shape...thick in the middle, curved back and forth its entire length, its slim legs reaching in various directions, grasping for whatever purchase they can find. The shapes of new voting districts were reminiscent of these features. The salamander also provides the sense of the practice's slithery intellectual integrity, ever changeable. The majority of states in the U.S are currently governed by members of the Republican Party. They understand the advantages of staying in office, and are gerrymandering voting districts with ultra-sophisticated polling information that is granular down to the individual voter's every political meander. If you are a Republican, you're in, at least for the moment; if Democrat, you're a good deal less in.

One last effort to restrict voting to a certain few is that of claiming that voter fraud is a regular and widespread practice throughout the country. Voter restriction is a favored philosophy by many who are afraid that immigrants and people of color in general are voting illegally, and thus unduly influencing the outcomes of elections. This has proven repeatedly not to be so, and only serves to open the door to the invasion of privacy of those who are suspected of being election scofflaws. Generally their color, religion and/or place of birth are what qualify them to be accused of voter fraud.

It used to be that the largest single group in the United States to be affected by such measures was the black community. The shackling of their influence was enshrined within the institution of slavery, and also by Article 1, Section 2 of the U.S Constitution, which has to do in part with how the population was to be counted, for the purposes of determining taxes for each particular state and figuring how many representatives could be elected from each state to the House of Representatives. This article made the un-free black person the equivalent of three-fifths of a white person. Of course, even after the Thirteenth Amendment outlawing slavery was passed, these people were forbidden to vote in many states, three-fifths, five-fifths or whatever.

There have been, to be sure, a few other ethnic groups that have been legislated against because of their supposed deleterious influence on the larger white majority: American Indians, subjected to massive pogroms and forced re-location to western reservations; Chinese, held in check by Chinese exclusionary laws in the nineteenth century; Japanese-American U.S. citizens and the World War II concentration camps in which they were imprisoned; and a large smattering of other, various "colored" populations. Even the occasional white subgroup has thus been affected, although it would be laughable to lump them in with these others, simply because they do indeed remain white. But the Irish, for example, were so odd and threatening with their unruliness and mumbo-jumbo Catholicism that they were quite clearly discriminated against by mainstream white Protestant Americans until well into the late-nineteenth century. (As a very young man, the author's grandfather, born in Chicago in the 1880s, was turned away from possible employment by the suggestion in various shop window signs and newspaper job announcements that "No Irish Need Apply." He spoke English with an American accent; but his name was Mike Brennan.) The discrimination the Irish suffered, especially if fresh off the boat, was in any case temporary because, as long as he or she did not speak in that peculiar, humorous way they have, they could disappear into the white majority population.

In any case, it is no longer simply a matter principally of Blacks and Whites. During the years since the 1970s, massive shifts in immigration patterns to the United States have caused a much more diverse population to evolve in this country. Now there are Asians of every sort, Africans from everywhere across that continent, Indians, Pakistanis, Central and South Americans, more western Europeans, more eastern Europeans. And of course more attention is being paid now to the situation for native Americans (the Standing Rock Sioux, for one example, and their objections to the Dakota Access oil pipeline,) who are hardly immigrants at all... or perhaps better said, were the very first immigrants.

The cultural differences that were etched in such clear relief by the Civil Rights movement have now been multiplied immeasurably. While our society was once for the most part "white" or "black," now this country has become a polyglot, poly-cultural phenomenon of such extraordinary complexity that the multiplicity can be seen and heard clearly simply by walking down a crowded city street almost anywhere in the U.S.

Until very recently, this expansion of cultural diversity was a mark of the American ideal. The United States is after all a nation built upon immigration. The sophistication and learning that clearly comes with the influx of new cultures and ideas seemed to be, if not lauded by Americans themselves, at least considered by them. It goes without saying, though, that those millions of immigrants have benefitted from the American experience, whether they have been openly welcomed or not.

But in the election of the current president, a new backlash against such diversity had formidable support among conservative white voters. Despite their candidate's having been summarily defeated in the 2016 popular vote, they now appear to be using their electoral college victory as a mandate to regress to a version of American nativism similar to that which held sway in 1972...and earlier.

The most startling evidence of this wish is embodied in the events in Charlottesville, Virginia on August 11 and 12, 2017. On the night of the eleventh, a large group of so-called "alt-right" demonstrators paraded across the campus of the University of Virginia, carrying lit torches reminiscent of those favored by the Ku Klux Klan. They chanted various mantras: "Jews will not replace us!"; "White lives matter!"; "We want our country back!" and so on. Allegedly protesting the planned removal of a statue of

Confederate General Robert E. Lee, they used the occasion also to make clear their belief that white people have cultural and political ascendancy in the United States, always have had it, and deserve that to be so.

The following day, groups of armed and armored white nationalists carrying placards and shouting slogans reminiscent of the symbols and speech of Hitler's Germany descended upon Charlottesville itself. Ersatz swastikas, shouts of "Blood and soil!" et. al. A street battle ensued between these people and others who were alarmed by the treacherous appearance of what were clearly neo-Nazi sentiments and actions. Eventually, one woman was killed and several others injured.

The president's claim that both sides were equally responsible for the violence avoids mention of the association of the alt-right in general with Nazism. Anyone who lived through that era, or who has a reasonable understanding of its history and of the war that was fought to eradicate it, clearly understands where the president got it wrong.

—

It has now been more than forty years since the last session of the class "Human Conflict" was held. All the students have gone on with their lives, married and founded families, gone through entire careers, retired, traveled…and considered, in the case of almost all the former students interviewed, what "Human Conflict: Black and White" meant to them.

Clifford observed something in the 1990s that has real application now. "You know, the skinheads and the hatred that is rising now…even some Blacks are rising again in this way. When a group of people of a certain rank are suppressed, and other people are excelling and have money, the racial issue becomes a rallying point."

An irony has surfaced in recent years. Clifford's "skinheads," (whom I take to mean mostly white people with little education) now feel that they are the class being oppressed in this country. Their problems have come about because of the tremendous disruptive developments in recent years in the high-tech industries. Actual manufacturing jobs continue disappearing at an alarming rate, and those white people who used to fill those jobs are finding themselves threatened and, prior to the election of Donald Trump as president, ignored. A working class that once willy-nilly excluded people of color is now being excluded itself...or so they think. But while these people once had the legal system on their side, they are now suffering from a breakdown in education—and their own nonchalance when it comes to re-educating themselves—that leaves them untrained and unprepared for the current world.

Because these are the people who constitute the largest single voting bloc for the current president, it makes sense that his rhetoric and policies so often brim with white nativist yearnings and the re-institution of restriction and punishment of non-white others.

Pete Kranz has a solution. "A course like 'Human Conflict' should be mandatory at universities today, given the current controversies stemming from race. I would teach it in the same way. No holds barred."

Patty, a white woman who was a home host for Pete's UNF class, takes a pragmatic view of what could be offered: "I think the class should be offered to high school kids, preferably freshmen. The younger the better. By college, students are pretty well formed. Whites and Blacks both still have a long way to go when it comes to changing attitudes. Bigotry still is rampant on both sides."

One of the black home hosts addressed the complications of new im-migrations to the U.S. in a recent interview. "There is more violence in the black communities now for sure, and it is getting that way in the white communities. We have lots of different people from all over the world. Cubans, Puerto Ricans, Muslims, Indians from India...everywhere. And every community is identifying itself as a separate entity."

Those separate entities are defined by ethnicity, culture and, at the very center, race. As Price Cobbs writes in the foreword to this book, "Race is the one circumstance that pertains to all Americans... [In our racial confrontation groups] we had found irrevocably that to pussyfoot around race in any such discussion is to ignore the single most important element of them all."

The divide between black and white people still represents the largest one in the culture of the United States, because of the history that derived from it and drove so much of our structure of laws and our current culture. One conclusion of many of the former students we have interviewed is that the racial divide is in many ways worse now than it was even in the early 1970s. This is not a universal opinion, but the frequency with which it is uttered does not come as a surprise to any of the former students. With the revival of voting registration limitations in many states, the obvious gerry-mandering of innumerable voting districts, strongly worded anti-immigrant rhetoric, the threats to immigrants already living here who have gotten U.S. citizenship and are nonetheless being discriminated against…with all this, the influence of minority voting blocs is being attacked in ways clearly reminiscent—especially to black people—of Jim Crow legislations. As a result, a number of the former students interviewed have the opinion that now is the time to re-institute "Human Conflict: Black and White." "If everyone in the United States were to undergo a class like that," one of the former students says, "there would be much less such division and far more cooperation between Blacks, Whites and everyone else."

The many new arrivals from everywhere would be included. Harold feels this to be a must. "It should be a requirement for everybody going to a formal education. But especially in certain fields, it should be a core course because we have so many problems of a racial nature now. It isn't just black and white. There's this Korean, that Syrian, this Somali, that Venezuelan." The differences they represent to nativist Whites in this country are under close, angry scrutiny by those Whites. The Human Conflict method and practices are intended for these immigrants also, and would serve them well…as they would the white nationalists themselves.

In these times, though, such a course could be difficult to present at institutions of higher learning in the United States. Political correctness runs rampant in a great many of those schools, and the notion of the uni-versity as a democratic ideal where divergent points of view can be freely presented and then debated seems quite threatened…despite the fact that such debate should be one of the unquestioned *raisons d'être* of the univer-sity. The ease with which Pete Kranz was able to get the UNF staff to agree to his course could be difficult now. Litigation, objections from donors and alumni, campus riot, and the fear that those possibilities instill in the hearts of university administrations, would possibly make even the suggestion of such a course controversial and subject to dismissal. This could be so especially once the administrators were to realize that confrontation, racial intensities, shouting, anger, violent language, and truth-telling were to be the essence of the course. No matter that these elements, properly monitored, are precisely what made the UNF classes so successful. In those classes, political correctness was stripped away, and forthright honesty, no matter how difficult, was uniformly insisted upon. Racism was thoroughly addressed, in detail after detail, white and black, no matter the hurt feelings or embarrassment that may have resulted, and successfully dealt with.

But now, the clear evidence of respect for each other and the fellow feeling that resulted from the UNF classes may account for little in any attempt to re-instate those classes. A climate of timidity further worsened by the possibility of violence pervades the administrative offices of many of these institutions.

"Even with today's more litigious society, though," Pete Kranz says, "it still would be very worth trying. There may be risks involved with innovative formats, where required student interaction takes place outside the protection of the classroom. We would likely have to receive approval from university legal counsel and have signed acceptance of certain terms and conditions for participation, from faculty, students and host families. But the rewards could well justify the risks. After all, the classes worked."

To that end, at this writing, Pete, who is on the faculty now of the University of Texas, visits numerous colleges and universities stating his case for what happened in his time at UNF, and why what he and those students did makes a clear case for re-visiting the entire idea as an educational opportunity of real value.

Educational institutions are not the only possibility, however. Corporate business, religious organizations, medical institutions, governmental bodies, organizations devoted to the social good...all manner of other opportunities for such confrontation groups exist. Given the remarkable success of those small gatherings in the 1970s, these institutions would do well to explore the possibilities of racial confrontation as a way to insure racial peace.

A Last Word

None of those who participated in these classes ever claimed that they were easy. But the personal pain encountered was more often than not accompanied by deep personal respect for each other. Shouts brought on fellow feeling. Rage expressed brought about the possibility for respect offered and even love felt.

Patricia, a black student, writes about this in her journal. "Sometimes I feel so drained of all emotion that I'm at a standstill. It's like when the others hurt, I hurt, whether I like it or not, and I feel like screaming and screaming. Then when I get in class, I get the extra boost that makes me want to keep going."

Reflecting on his six years having officiated at these meetings and having witnessed all the rough things said, Pete Kranz is unequivocal in his thoughts about the results. He pauses in his conversation, to take in a breath. "This was in every way a positive intervention." He has no doubt that, with the "conversations about race" that Price Cobbs describes, and the "eggshell discussions" that resulted, resulting in such slight improvement in the root difficulties of racism, the methods embodied by "Human Conflict: Black and White" are the keys to a solution that has remained hidden throughout the history of race relations in the United States.

AUTHOR'S NOTE

There are two former students from the class "Human Conflict: Black and White" without whose insights I would have had great difficulty writing this book.

Judi Benson is the "Judi" about whom I write in the book, and she provided me with four hundred-plus pages of word-processed notes that she had gathered together and organized, based on her own experiences in the class and (more to the point of the variety of experience in those groups) the journals that so many of the students freely gave to Pete Kranz on the last day of their particular semester. This document from Judi contained all of the comments from the various student journals that are included in this book, as well as the transcriptions of follow-up conversations that Pete had with many of the students in 1993. (I too gathered information in 2017, from personal interviews with some of the students, to whom I am grateful.) Making a clear-eyed, smooth and organized document from all these different sources was a formidable task for Judi because of the great number of them, and of how thoughtful the participants were. I could not have succeeded in my task were it not for her work.

The other student is Ann Hurst. She is the "Ann" whom I quote frequently in this book. Her journals were copious, well written, always direct, and very self-revealing. She and Judi were in the same edition of the class, and Judi says of her, "She proved to be the toughest on me, on us all, and I thank her for that. It is no wonder I remember her most, and why we became friends.... Even those who took exception to Ann's outspokenness eventually came around to understanding what she was about, that she was there partly to rile things up."

Almost all the journals have significant moments of introspection, but Ann's journal is always introspective. Indeed, the one person on whom she is the toughest is herself. I would have enjoyed interviewing her, but learned on the day in 2016 that Pete Kranz first introduced me to many of these former students, that Ann had passed away just a few weeks before. Her assumptions about the value of the class, and her determination to make its goals be realized, taught me how successful the whole methodology of "racial confrontation" can be.

Finally, Dr. Price M. Cobbs was a very willing consultant to me throughout the writing of this book. As *An Arena of Truth* was being prepared for publication in June 2018, Price passed away at the age of eighty-nine. His efforts with Dr. William H. Grier to close the racial divide in the U.S. through use of racial confrontation groups was essential to Pete Kranz's work at the University of North Florida. Price's co-authorship with Bill Grier of *Black Rage* would have sufficed admirably as a helpmate to Pete's classes in the 1970s. But Price's personal influence on Pete's early design of those classes was key. Price went on through the rest of his life to foster similar ideas and methods in his very significant work in opening corporate America to aspiring black executives (men and women) at every level. For all these accomplishments, Price Cobbs deserves truly special thanks.

—Terence Clarke

About Terence Clarke

Publisher, editor, novelist (Mercury House, Ballantine Books), short-story writer (*The Yale Review, The Antioch Review, The Chariton Review, Denver Quarterly, Tampa Review, Kindle Singles* and others), journalist (*San Francisco Chronicle, Salon.com, Huffington Post*), and translator of poetry, fiction, and narrative non-fiction from Spanish to English, Terence Clarke is the author of nine books. His critically acclaimed novels include *My Father in the Night, The King of Rumah Nadai, A Kiss for Señor Guevara, The Notorious Dream of Jesús Lázaro,* and *The Splendid City.* He has written three short-story collections: *The Day Nothing Happened, Little Bridget and the Flames of Hell,* and *New York.* He is co-founder and director of publishing at Astor & Lenox in San Francisco.

—

If you find this book of value, please consider writing a customer review of it for your local bookstore or on the book's page at the online site from which you purchased it.

CPSIA information can be obtained
at www.ICGtesting.com
Printed in the USA
LVHW040745030520
654647LV00002B/146

9 781732 919501